TYRANNY IN AMERICA

TYRANNY IN AMERICA

Capitalism and National Decay

NEAL WOOD

VERSO

London • New York

First published by Verso 2004
© Neal Wood
All rights reserved

1 3 5 7 9 10 8 6 4 2

Verso
UK: 6 Meard Street, London w1f 0eg
USA: 180 Varick Street, New York, ny 10014–4606
www.versobooks.com

Verso is the imprint of New Left Books

ISBN 1–85984–572–X

British Library Cataloguing in Publication Data
Wood Neal
    Tyranny in America : capitalism and national decay
    1. Capitalism – United States 2. Capitalism – Social aspects
    – United States 3. National characteristics, American
    4. United States – Politics and government – 1989 – 5. United
    States – Social conditions – 1980 –
    I. Title
    320.9′73′09051

ISBN 185984572X

Library of Congress Cataloging-in-Publication Data
Wood, Neal.
    Tyranny in America : capitalism and national decay / Neal Wood.
        p. cm.
    ISBN 1-85984-572-X (cloth : alk. paper)
    1. Capitalism–Moral and ethical aspects–United States. 2. United
States–Moral conditions. 3. Social problems–United States. 4. United
States–Social conditions. I. Title.
    HN90.M6W66 2004
    306′.0973–dc22

                                                    2003024367

Typeset in Minion by YHT Ltd, London
Printed in the UK by William Clowes

To those throughout the world who have
so courageously and so long struggled against
capitalist oppression, and to its countless victims.

CONTENTS

Neal Wood died on 17 September 2003, just as this book was going through the last stages of production. So this, the most fiercely polemical work in his long and distinguished scholarly career, will be his last. That seems a fitting testimony to the fighting spirit and the implacable opposition to injustice that characterized him till the end.

PREFACE

Quite obviously, this short book is not a rigorous intellectual analysis with a complex apparatus of footnotes. Rather, it is a somewhat impassioned and impressionistic essay motivated by my deep concern over advanced capitalism's pernicious effect upon our world. Part I, setting the scene, as it were, for Part II, is a brief excursion into the 'history of ideas' that attempts to outline in abbreviated fashion the inversions of the concepts of *avarice* and *democracy* in the past few centuries, inversions to my mind absolutely crucial for an under-standing of the tyranny of capitalism over America in the twenty-first century. Part II focuses upon the apparent decay of American society and politics now that avarice and democracy in their historically inverted forms underwrite capitalist tyranny. Here my intention is to deluge the reader with readily available facts and figures (gleaned from, among other sources, the *New York Times, International Herald Tribune, Guardian* and *Observer*), which when collated may be sufficient to support my argument. My only hope is that in the midst of the patriotic fervour, flag-waving and hubris following the catastrophe of 11 September 2001, which has drawn the US into the quagmire of Iraq, American readers will be brought down to earth, take stock of themselves and their country, and seriously reflect upon the military juggernaut they have unleashed upon humankind. And perhaps some readers of a scholarly disposition may see fit to accept or refute my thesis.

Apart from the classics of political theory and socialism, my thinking in writing this book has been shaped by numerous authors, especially by Albert O. Hirschman's *The Passions and the Interests* (1977), and by the works of friends and colleagues: Robert Brenner, *Merchants and Revolution* (1993); George Comninel, *Rethinking the French Revolution* (1987); David McNally, *Political Economy and the Rise of Capitalism* (1988); Colin Mooers, *The Making of Bourgeois Europe* (1991), and Ellen Meiksins Wood, *The Pristine Culture of Capitalism* (1991); *Democracy Against Capitalism* (1995) and *The Origin of Capitalism* (2002). Also of value has been Will Hutton's recent *The World We're In* (2002), although we disagree on a number of salient points.

Once again, I wish to express my profound gratitude to Ellen Meiksins Wood for reading several drafts, and for her invaluable criticisms, suggestions and supportive companionship over the years. I am deeply indebted to my old friend, Gordon J. Schochet of Rutgers University, for his exceedingly useful comments on an early version. Of course, neither is in any way responsible for what I say.

Finally, many thanks are also due to the indispensable fact-gathering of Atif Khan and Gibin Hong, graduate assistants in the Department of Political Science, York University, Toronto; and to the patient, painstaking typing and retyping of Edward Telesford of London and Jayne Woof of Chagford, Devon.

Neal Wood
London

1

DANGER AHEAD

Now that the horrible event of 11 September has occurred, and the United States under George W. Bush has launched its 'infinite war' on terrorism, after a spell of fervent patriotic flag-waving Americans may wish to pause for reflection and self-examination. They will come to realize that they are by no means the only people who ever have been or who are now exposed to terrorism, often more sustained, long-lasting and costly than the destruction of the World Trade Center and its employees. Nor should Americans forget that much of the terrorism throughout the world in the last decades has been unleashed and promoted by the United States and that they failed to make any protest. Examples of US-sponsored terrorism can be found in Africa, Latin America and even Afghanistan before the recent bombardment and invasion. Three thousand helpless innocents may have been slaughtered on that fateful September day in 2001, but Americans should always remember that unlike Europe and the Soviet Union they were quite insulated from Nazi terrorism in the Second World

War, in which several thousand British civilians lost their lives in less than a year owing to the terrorist attacks of the Nazi V1s and V2s. Nor should Americans forget the more than twenty million lives sacrificed by the Soviet Union to the Nazi onslaught. Now that Afghanistan and Iraq have been subjected to relentless bombing by the United States, it has been estimated that some 2,000–8,000 non-combatants have been killed in the former and at least 5,000–10,000 in the latter, not counting the numerous others who have died of starvation. Can these attacks by the United States possibly be called the reasoned response of a mature people, or are they callous and unprincipled acts of revenge and imperialism? Not least, Americans should always remember that in addition to their fomenting of terrorism through-out the world, they have exacerbated the hatred of many by not taking bold positive steps to decrease appreciably the poverty and disease plaguing millions of the world's unfortunates, or to improve their educational standards.

Is it possible that the world's most advanced and powerful capitalist country, the United States of America, is slowly decaying and may ultimately break down? Is it possible that the United States is a sick society with a vacuous politics and antiquated structure of government on the verge of a terminal illness? Most readers, especially Americans, will answer these queries with a resounding and emphatic 'no', and may express serious reservations about the sanity of the questioner. For it should be understood from the outset that many Americans, despite the global travels of some (only a fraction hold passports), constant exposure to movies and TV, and the ongoing immigration of a sizeable number from foreign lands, seem so self-centred, so isolated from the rest of the world, so captivated by their dominant consumer culture, and so in thrall to capitalist ideology, that they lack any perspective on what is happening to them, their society and their polity. Seldom do they stand back and take stock of themselves and where they are going. Self-examination and self-criticism are not the American way. How can the United States – they will invariably respond with supreme confidence and utter lack of self-doubt – the most successful capitalist nation on earth, without peer or rival, at the same time be a decaying society? Since the collapse of the Soviet empire, the Cold War's end, and the globalization of capitalism, the United States has emerged without rival, a global economic and political colossus, the envied model for the rest of humankind. What evidence can possibly testify to any serious symptoms of decay in the United States? The obvious and unquestioned facts clearly speak for themselves, or so we are told.

Yet in spite of these stalwart defences of the status quo, something appears to be amiss in contemporary America, paradoxically at the zenith of its undeniable and spectacular accomplishments. Whether this is only a momentary aberration or temporary indisposition, or something of a more deep-rooted, sinister and permanent nature, remains to be seen. At least, however, we should be alerted to some of the symptoms of the afflictions to which capitalist America could very well succumb.

We know that all great world empires throughout history – ancient Rome immediately comes to mind – have eventually declined and disintegrated. The decay has usually come from within. Will capitalist America be the sole exception to this apparently inevitable fate, to what seems to be an iron law of history? We are told in response that this is sheer delusion, a highly simplistic and grossly distorted view of both past and present. Obviously, an unbridgeable gulf separates contemporary America from ancient Rome, for example. It may be pointed out that qualitatively, the world has changed so much since classical antiquity that this analogy is rendered completely incongruous, if not farcical. The most palpable and insurmountable difference between these two world empires, apart from a distance of nearly two millennia of history, is America's advanced capitalist economy and highly developed and sophisticated technology that affects the lives of the entire global population. So at the most simplistic level it is not even a case of comparing apples and oranges.

But the fact remains that all unchallenged imperial orders have been subject to degeneration, and that an advanced capitalist society may by no means be immune to collapse. Indeed, advanced capitalism and technology may simply accelerate, intensify and expand the process of decay. At the very time that the sickness commences, capitalism and technology could by their very nature successfully conceal it for an indefinite period from the countless participants and even from astute detached observers. In the past, the existence of a single supreme military, political and economic world power without imminent threat to its own survival and domination has in the long term led to self-destruction. When this unrivalled global giant is also capitalist and technologically advanced, the course of social decay may very well gather pace while remaining hidden for an appreciable interval from the common view.

The advanced capitalist organization of society, or so I argue in this book, contains within itself the seeds of its own annihilation. This is absolutely central to the inherent nature of capitalism, at least as we have experienced it. Capitalism is much more than a fundamentally economic phenomenon, because it profoundly affects the totality of human relations. The persistence and success of these relations in the final analysis rest on the basic beliefs and cherished values of the actors themselves. They include not only employers and entrepreneurs but also, and this is of absolutely critical importance, the innumerable women and men involved in the whole complex system, employees, managers, technicians and consumers; in short, all who live and work in capitalist society.

The flourishing of any form of social organization, not only capitalism, depends ultimately on the support of its members. Their buttressing beliefs furnish the authoritative underpinning and necessary motor of all societies. Advanced capitalism in the United States (and other powerful and successful capitalist countries) is justified and nurtured by a widely held, seldom questioned, and vigorous set of views and values that constitute the *capitalist mentality* or mind set, an ideological prime mover and sustainer.

The capitalist mentality must be identified and defined if we are to assess the possibility of an American social breakdown some time in the future. Today most of us take capitalism for granted, and our outlook and behaviour which are shaped by it seem natural and inherent. From birth to the end of our lives we are so habituated to capitalist society (and the sustaining beliefs and attitudes upon which they are founded and by which they thrive) that we cannot imagine how things might be other than they are. But this may be simple self-delusion and obfuscation of the actual state of affairs.

1

To transcend such blinding false consciousness we sorely require the illumination of history, 'witness of the times' and 'light of truth', as Cicero long ago described it. Concentrated as we are on ourselves in the present, we tend to be oblivious to the past and its cultures and societies. Any understanding of our own predicament, any critical self-knowledge through historical reflection, seem beyond our capabilities and interests. Yet if the historical record is probed, we soon come to realize that capitalism and the capitalist mentality are of very recent origin. Capitalism, much less the capitalist organization of entire societies, has not always been with us. Nor has capitalism even in rudimentary form existed throughout the span of western civilization, only to be freed suddenly in the modern era from impediments to its full development. Capitalism is not the age-old propensity to 'buy cheap and sell dear', so typical of bazaar and market-place since time immemorial, that has somehow been liberated from all restrictions and emancipated in the last few centuries.

On the contrary, capitalism is a unique historical development, which arose and, at first, evolved very slowly under quite specific circumstances from an unprecedented conjunction of geographical, social, political and cultural factors. Initially, capitalism appeared and began to make inroads in the sixteenth-century English agrarian sector and there alone; later it gradually permeated commerce and industry. Over three centuries later, Britain became the first industrial capitalist nation, symbolized by the opening of the Crystal Palace Exhibition of London in 1851, so close to us in time that the grandparents of some of those alive today were alive then. Since that relatively recent date, capitalism has swept western Europe and North America, and has now become a gargantuan economic force throughout the world. Capitalism, in other words, has existed for only a minute fraction of the lengthy story of human society and even of the mere 5,000-year lifetime of the organized state. So we should never deceive ourselves into believing that capitalism and capitalist materialism are essentially natural to humankind or inherent in the human make-up, nor should we ever take them for granted.

Historical knowledge of what preceded capitalism and the capitalist mentality, focusing on differences as well as similarities, may enhance our appreciation of the novelty and uniqueness of our thinking and actions today. Historical ignorance obscures some of the most significant features of current life, blinding us to critical self-knowledge. A particular society and culture flow out of the accumulated experience and social construction of previous peoples and cultures. We are as we are because of all that has happened before us. Humans and their societies are the artefacts of history. We act as we do through existing institutions and arrangements because we and they have been moulded by the historical process. Our thoughts and actions should never be accepted, without incisive reflection, as being natural or innate to our make-up. A study of history sensitizes us to what joins us to, as well as divides us from, our predecessors. We add, as it were, the next floor to the structure built by our forebears, and the character of the new addition depends in no small part on the configuration of the lower floors. Reflection on the past is a liberating endeavour, launching us on the path to self-discovery. In this enterprise, our beliefs and values will alter, both consciously and unconsciously. We make and remake ourselves through the constant assessment and reassessment of the past. Historical understanding, from this perspective, can also be socially subversive, pressing us to reconsider what we have so often taken for granted, leading us to question existing institutions and arrangements and to search for alternatives to the status quo. This is why serious historical study can be a thorn in the flesh of the powers that be and is often discouraged.

The enlightening experience of studying history changes us and our views, and consequently has a direct bearing upon the way we fashion the future. Seen in this way, the past is the intermediary between present and future, a causeway linking the two. Nevertheless, we should always be cautious that what is learned from the past is not applied mechanically, like a blueprint for building the future. Instead, the past as an invaluable instrument of critical self-understanding may shed light on the direction we are taking. If we dislike that direction, careful scrutiny of the past can suggest others. Humans are not hapless victims of the past, to be propelled along a road they do not wish to take. Admittedly, the past limits our options, but we can usually seize the initiative, and as the creators of history ourselves, we need not be the helpless playthings of fortune. Obviously, we think and act within the limits imposed by the past. But within these bounds, choices can be made to our advantage and benefit, so long as we do not lose our nerve but act with courage and determination, with knowledge imposed by hindsight and foresight. Our actions must be conscious and rational, with comprehension of the full range of choices and their possible consequences, illuminated by the Ciceronian 'light of truth' shed by the constant beacon of historical understanding and reflection.

I have no intention of exploring economic history and the development of capitalism. Many others, much better qualified than I, have done this or are doing it. Rather, by way of introduction, in Part I, I shall touch on a few traits of the *pre-capitalist* mentality in the hope of alerting readers to the astonishing inversion of values that has occurred in England, the original heartland of capitalism, since the Middle Ages. This truly revolutionary transformation of belief slowly arose with the gradual emergence of English capitalism. The shift in attitudes was a response to the emerging society, lagging somewhat behind its development. These new values have reached fruition in the early twenty-first century as capitalism has proliferated throughout the world, thriving especially in the United States since the mid-nineteenth-century Civil War, where they have become the crucial mental foundation, rationale and motor of advanced capitalist society. Only when we begin to understand the amazing inversion of beliefs that has occurred in the previous centuries, first little by little and then with rising momentum, will we be able to estimate the possible extent of a serious malady afflicting American society.

My efforts to plot the historical course of the capitalist mentality will be confined to Chapters 2 and 3, which cover selected aspects of ancient and mediaeval thought, and early modern social and political ideas, particularly in England. The focus will be on two of the most important conceptual changes: first, attitudes to *avarice*, or greed for money and possessions, and their effects on social unity; second, attitudes to *democracy* and its relationship to the former. Think of the radical implications in the basic alteration of the traditionally negative attitudes towards avarice, on the one hand, and democracy, on the other. These are, possibly, the major ideological shifts that enabled advanced capitalism to dominate the world. In the pre-capitalist era from classical antiquity, both avarice and democracy were widely thought to threaten social unity and to be destructive of it. Then as capitalism emerged and blossomed during the last few centuries, avarice was gradually legitimized, and eventually came to be considered the basis, not the destroyer, of social harmony and order; likewise the notion of democracy, which by the opening of the twenty-first century was judged to be the primary goal and guarantor of social solidarity. In the ideological sphere capitalism welded the two together: a newly clothed avarice and a disfigured conception of democracy. Together, indeed, they have become the heart and soul of capitalist ideology, absorbed by the capitalist mentality, forming a unique, inseparable and indispensable bolstering motive force.

Then, to proceed with my agenda, some transitional comments in Chapter 4 will be made on my distinction between the old notion of tyranny and the new capitalist tyranny. In Part II, Chapters 5 and 6 will be devoted to some of the social and political developments brought about by advanced capitalism and its new tyranny over the United States. But to conclude the present chapter, some attempt is in order at delineating the capitalist mentality.

2

The archetype of the capitalist mentality existing today in the United States, and to a lesser degree in other advanced capitalisms, is essentially a composite of a *rationalizing ideology* and an *energizing ideology*. The first consists of the ideas and ideals justifying capitalism and capitalist behaviour to which the newly fashioned conception of democracy is central. This more obvious ideology of rationalization tends to camouflage the less obvious energizing ideology enshrining avarice that is the driving force, the dynamo of capitalism. Each of these components of the capitalist mentality will be briefly explained in what follows.

We are all familiar with the loudly proclaimed and highly publicized justification for capitalist endeavour. Capitalism and the free market are now closely linked to democracy, and sometimes even identified with democracy. Corporate enterprise, the media and politicians constantly remind us that capitalism and democracy are inseparable. Even school and university classrooms are deluged with these blandishments. Capitalism, we are never allowed to forget in authoritative pronouncements, means ever greater freedom of the individual, especially ever expanding freedom of choice for the consumer, rendered possible by the free market and minimal government intervention. A shameless distortion of Adam Smith's great *Wealth of Nations* (1776) has become the bible of these ideologues, as we see in Chapter 2. Not only does capitalism endow the individual with ever greater liberty, which is labelled the core of democracy, but in addition, capitalism rests on juridical and legal equality, another much vaunted characteristic of democracy. Furthermore, capitalism is a mode of social organization according to merit. The most hard-working and able will ultimately reach the top of the social pyramid, becoming managers and key decision-makers in the economic, social and political hierarchy. In sum, advanced capitalist society is a democratic meritocracy. Everyone in a properly ordered capitalist society has an equal opportunity to rise to the pinnacle of power, prestige and influence. Capitalist society, therefore, is the realm of opportunity, *par excellence*. Those who climb to the summit of capitalism do so on the basis of merit, perseverance and industry, not because of family, ancestry, income, sex, race or good luck. Capitalist society, hence, is a democratic, egalitarian and classless society. Moreover, capitalist society is constantly changing for the better, perpetually growing and improving. Progress is its indelible hallmark. So the ideals of *democracy*, *individualism*, *freedom*, *equality*, *merit*, *opportunity*, *classlessness* and *progress* are the crucial values by which capitalism is justified and promoted. The message is broadcast to the world, urging others to follow suit and join the march to the Promised Land.

Thus the proponents and ideologues of advanced American capitalism proudly proclaim its advantages and benefits to a largely captive mass audience, and do so with astounding certainty in the conviction that they cannot possibly be mistaken. They are the true believers in capitalism who with messianic fervour foresee a veritable paradise on earth, if only everyone holds to the course, no matter the hardships encountered along the way. Throughout their lives the American people and much of the rest of the world are bombarded with this fabrication of untruths and half-truths, enunciated by absolutely confident and never-doubting new utopians. Without widespread and deep beliefs in these myths, advanced capitalist society as we know it could never survive, grow stronger and expand. Without them capitalist society might very well collapse and wither away.

Much less misleading and beguiling than these rationalizing beliefs of the capitalist mentality is the ideology driving them, usually masterfully disguised by them. Here we enter the sphere of avarice (as we see in Chapter 2), so long condemned, and now rendered respectable, the centrepiece of the whole capitalist enterprise. Here we are confronted with the viciousness and brutality of capitalist values, capitalism red in tooth and claw, in all its nakedness, stripped of the adulatory sloganeering of justification. Rarely articulated in all its crudity and predatory parasitism, extreme capitalist ideology is probably held consciously by relatively few: those who by deceit and craft are out for a 'fast buck' or an enormously profitable killing, or outright cynics striving to reap enormous profits, those who know the score, living for the present and damning the consequences for themselves and their fellow humans. Held in varying degrees by others at all levels of society, here nevertheless is the essence of the capitalist mentality, the animus of capitalist activity driving it ever onwards, and possibly to its eventual breakdown and destruction.

Engaging in a brief thought experiment may help in delineating the ideology driving the capitalist mentality. Imagine for a moment that we are given the task of creating an entirely new society according to any design we choose. We begin with a *tabula rasa*, human raw material, like the hero-founders in the ancient myths of classical antiquity. Given this immense and challenging project of social engineering, where do we begin and how do we proceed? What kind of society shall we build?

Imagine that we establish our society on the basis of the rudiments of the dynamics of advanced capitalist America, stripped down to the bare essentials and without any justificatory ideology. We would be engaged in constructing something that would be neither 'society' nor 'state' as commonly understood. Our social engineer or hero-founder would succeed only in producing a collection of atomistic individuals whose sole standard is the free range of their desires, with the desires of the strongest and cleverest prevailing. Each of these atomistic bundles of desire engages in ruthless competitive struggle with the others, all pursuing their own self-interest and pleasure, maximizing their accumulation of money and possessions, and free apart from minimal restraints. The dynamic of this aggregate of disparate and contending individuals is the idea that security, pleasure and happiness depend upon greed and the pleasure acquired from riches. Legitimate self-interest would soon be replaced by avaricious selfishness. This conflux of profit-seeking human atoms is little more than a variation on the Hobbesian theme of the state of nature, in fact a state of war of all against all, in which the shrewdest and most driven worshippers of money survive to dominate and subject the less astute and more innocent. All that is distinctly human is soon sacrificed on the altar of mammon. Any cohesion among the warring competitors shortly fragments and disintegrates because of the centrifugal forces unleashed by rampant materialism at the behest of untrammelled desire. The process of decomposition, of course, might for a while be concealed from the actors themselves and delayed by a sedulously cultivated justificatory ideology that their behaviour is normal and natural, the realization of the human essence, and the fulfilment of its professed values. The day of reckoning, however, cannot be indefinitely postponed, even by the most artful ideological manipulation.

One might strenuously object – and with some reason – to all this, even as a thought experiment, as being at best little more than the grossest of caricatures. Although such a portrayal of the motive force of capitalism should, perhaps, not be taken too literally, much of it nevertheless seems to capture something of the fundamental nature of the capitalist way of life, the generator of capitalist society. Nor should we forget that neoliberalism typified by Reaganism and Thatcherism explicitly invoked aspects of this outlook. Occasionally the essence of human behaviour is tellingly suggested by even the most monstrous of caricatures. For instance, a caricature of contemporary capitalist

America is at present being most painfully constructed in post-communist Russia with the effort to build a free-market, democratic, capitalist society in a nation without historical experience of any of these things, much less of a culture receptive to them. This ill-conceived project has had the tragic consequences of untold human suffering, dreadful loss of human dignity, and destruction of the social fabric. The recent continuing restructuring of Russia is obviously a magnified and distorted reflection of what may be happening in American capitalist society, telling us something about what the future could hold for the United States itself.

The absolutely vital problem to be examined throughout the following is comprehended by at least two questions. First, can a society premised on avarice and self-seeking, albeit disguised as democracy, possibly cohere in the long run as a viable enterprise? This is of critical concern, particularly in light of the fact that the United States dominates the globe without any immediate threat to its supremacy. Second, does such a society contain within itself the seeds of its eventual destruction and demise?

Part I

THE CAPITALIST MENTALITY

AVARICE DISGUISED AND LEGITIMIZED

In the pre-capitalist era widespread greed for money and possessions was excoriated and believed to be the principal cause of social and political fragmentation and decay. Such an outlook will astonish many of us, conditioned as we are to capitalism and so captivated by its values that we accept without thought or reservation individual profit-seeking and property accumulation as a matter of course, the natural way of life. Perhaps, however, we should become historically aware: the unrestrained pursuit of riches was invariably condemned by moralists and commentators until about 1500, some two thousand years after the apogee of ancient Greek culture. Avarice and social disunity were the fearsome twins for ancient and mediaeval thinkers. Then, from the time of the early Renaissance, a remarkable change of attitude begins. An all but forgotten sixteenth-century English writer, Sir Thomas Smith, notably contributed to this change. By the eighteenth century's end, the age-old moral antipathy to greed and unbridled acquisition of wealth had, with some exceptions, withered away. Three British thinkers of the eighteenth century – David Hume, Adam Smith and Edmund Burke – were prominent figures in this striking transformation of values.

1

In ancient Greece and Rome whenever increasing personal fortunes were being amassed and economic inequalities were burgeoning, avarice was dreaded by thinkers as a threat to social unity. Plato, as in so many other instances, was among the first to denounce avarice, writing in *The Republic* of 'the money-loving spirit of sensual appetite', which like an Oriental potentate enslaves both reason and ambition. His disciple, Aristotle, while similarly denouncing money-making as an end in itself, raised no objection to the acquisition of riches when tempered by moderation and liberality. Two notable and exceedingly influential Roman thinkers, Cicero and Seneca, both well-to-do personages, followed suit. Uninhibited greed was anathema to Cicero, who claimed that 'the wise man alone is rich'. Nonetheless, he condoned acquisition if remaining within moral limits and used for virtuous ends. Seneca, one of the wealthiest dignitaries of the early empire and Nero's prime minister, dubbed avarice 'the mightiest curse of the human race', at the same time rationalizing his own great fortune in much the same way as Cicero before him had done with his more modest resources.

Christians were in the forefront of those who roundly denounced avarice. The Bible tells us that 'the love of money is the root of all evil', and that the true believer cannot serve both God and mammon. The father of Christian theology, St Augustine of Hippo, asserts that cupidity or love of money is one of the three pernicious lusts afflicting fallen man, a voracious appetite driving the individual on in a restless, perpetual and insatiable struggle for money and possessions, inciting a war of all against all. Christians regarded avarice as one of the seven deadly sins, deemed to be the deadliest by the end of the Middle Ages and, along with pride, the most subversive of vices. That second great figure of Christian theology, St Thomas Aquinas, adheres to Aristotle's position, believing that we should strive with moderation for money and possessions only in order to satisfy our needs, any excess being employed for worthy purposes. Avarice as an end in itself, St Thomas was convinced, demeans individuals and violates their humanity. When avarice becomes central to the lives of a people, other vices will spring up and rapidly proliferate. The result will be that deception and trickery soon replace mutual trust and friendship. A price will be set on everything and every person, the public good will be subordinated to private profit, and a once stable and peaceful political order and harmonious society will be riven by rampant selfishness, corruption and conflict.

From the late thirteenth century to the early fifteenth century a slow but perceptible erosion of the traditional antipathy to avarice and fear of its capacity to undermine social unity begins to appear in the writings of the Italian Renaissance humanists. Their changing sentiments may have reflected the boom in trade and commerce, and accompanying prosperity, of city-states like Florence, Venice and Milan, with the amassing of wealth by their thriving merchant families. The literati, often themselves prominent men of affairs, sometimes viewed the riches of citizens as a positive good instead of a menace to social order. Although the quest for fame and fortune might be hindered by avarice, it was also thought by some to advance the virtue of liberality (in keeping with the teachings of Aristotle and St Thomas), and to be conducive to happiness and its conservation. The acquisition of money through industry, initiative and business acumen, at least some believed, could contribute immeasurably to the well-being of the state and its citizens. Not the least consideration from this perspective was that private riches could succour a state in straitened circumstances. Such early modifications of the time-hallowed admonitions against avarice resonate in *On Avarice and Luxury* (1428–29) by Poggio Bracciolini, a future chancellor of the City of Florence: 'money is the nerve of life in a state, while those who have a love of money are the very foundation of the state itself'. His sentiment is far more in keeping with the 'modern spirit' than the distinctly 'old-fashioned' opinions of Machiavelli through whose words the political thought of Renaissance Italy is most familiar to many of us: 'well-ordered republics have to keep the public rich but their citizens poor' and 'poverty brings honour to cities, provinces, and religious institutions, whereas riches have ruined them'.

The new seeds sown by the humanists seem to have sprouted initially in England and later in France. English thought was possibly the first on this score because by the mid-sixteenth century only in England had incipient capitalism begun to take root, in the agrarian sector to be followed by commerce and industry in the subsequent centuries. The culmination of a 400-year process of development is that Great Britain by the mid-nineteenth century had become the world's first industrial capitalist nation.

A century after Bracciolini's chancellorship of Florence, in 1549 Sir Thomas Smith (1513–77) wrote a ground-breaking work, *A Discourse of the Commonweal of This Realm of England*, which circulated in manuscript and was finally published anonymously and posthumously in 1581. Little known today, Smith, once a student in Italy, Vice-Chancellor of Cambridge University and Provost of Eton College, was a Member of Parliament and an important official under King Edward VI and Queen Elizabeth I. In the form of a dialogue, the tome grappled with the serious problem of economic inflation afflicting England from the 1530s. Examining the cause of inflation and making recommendations for its remedy, Smith also touched upon the question of avarice and social order by situating the generalities of the Italian humanists in the concrete environment of emerging English agrarian capitalism (obviously unknown to him by this name).

Sir Thomas Smith's venture amounted to a Copernican revolution of the traditional moral condemnation of avarice as a danger to social unity. Writing from an essentially Augustinian position, he held that avaricious humans constantly strive to increase their pleasure and reduce their pain by increasing profits and cutting losses. In reflecting on practical matters of public policy and its implementation, he contends that any attempt to refashion humans, to try to remake them into what they are not and, to his mind, can never be, is certainly a fruitless and exceedingly perilous utopian task. Instead, we must, however reluctantly, resign ourselves to accepting humans as they actually are, with all their faults and frailties, their lusts and imperfections. The insatiable greed indelibly stamped on humans can in fact be harnessed to advance the common good, identified by Smith with the common interest, which he defines in terms of domestic peace, unity, security of person and possessions, and the well-being of all in accordance to their class, each individual pursuing profits as long as the profit-seeking of others is not hindered. By government's shrewd manipulation and prudent regulation, avarice can be prevented from destroying society and state, becoming rather its dynamic source of energy.

So, for instance, to cite Smith: if it is a question of two alternatives in agricultural policy, a less lucrative one responding to the common interest, the other allowing increased profits for a minority of greedy farmers, the 'occasion' for avarice must be removed from the second and allotted to the first. This can be accomplished by knowledgeable government intervention and clever management, for instance appropriate changes in taxation and customs duties. The result will be that the first alternative, clearly to the public advantage, will be rendered just as profitable to farmers as the second, if not more so. Avaricious farmers will consequently turn from the second to the first.

In analysing inflation, Smith makes several significant observations worth a passing mention. First, he stops just short of defining the 'economy' as an autonomous sphere possessing its own laws of motion propelled by human greed in a circular flow. Second, if the pursuit of profit is not to be socially divisive, the economic activities of individuals must be harmonized and directed towards the common interest by the informed policies of government, in the English case the existing Parliament of the chief profit-makers and their representatives, largely members of the landed upper classes. Thus he postulates an *artificial harmony of interests*, as distinct from Adam Smith's later conception of a *natural harmony of interests*. The differences between the two thinkers on this matter, however, as we shall see, are not as great as such a contrast at first glance implies. Third, Thomas Smith appears to suggest, if not explicitly argue, that production, distribution and exchange, originating in and driven by profit-orientated individuals organized through the social division of labour, comprise an indispensable integrative force within the state, though he never discounts the unity provided by the exercise of sovereign power in maintaining law and order. Furthermore, the centripetal compulsion of avarice canalized by the social division of labour is also a vital link among states, cementing friendship and peace in 'the common market of all the world'. Thomas Smith, therefore, evidently in response to some of the more socially divisive aspects of a fledgling capitalism making headway in England, foreshadowed a momentous shift in outlook that would become ever more prevalent and unquestioned.

The novelty of his approach is indicated by the fact that over two decades after he originally wrote the *Discourse*, the much more famous and influential French theorist, Jean Bodin, was still voicing the conventional distrust and condemnation of avarice, and one of his disciples bemoaned 'this monstrous Hydra of covetousness and lucre'. Nevertheless, the traditional moralizing was beginning to be challenged by others in France, for example by the illustrious essayist, Michel de Montaigne. In a piece published in 1580, he asserted that 'Greed can implant in the heart of a shop apprentice, brought up in obscurity and idleness, the confidence to cast himself far from hearth and home, in a frail boat at the mercy of waves and angry Neptune; it also teaches discretion and wisdom.' Still other Frenchmen were expanding on this theme of the social benefits of avarice, among them the minor dramatist Antoine de Montchrétien, who published the important *Treatise on Political Economy* in 1615, the first book employing the term in the title. His passion for economics, he confesses, was aroused by extended stays in Holland and England. While no evidence exists of his having read Smith's *Discourse*, his conclusions about avarice, human nature and the economy are remarkably similar to the Englishman's, the salient difference being his view that the artificial harmony of interests should be instituted and overseen by the French absolute monarch. Obviously, the vigorous moral condemnation of avarice over two millennia was crumbling, and a stress upon its social benefits was rapidly coming to the fore.

Capitalism, accelerating as the decades passed, was penetrating and shaping English society. Thomas Hobbes, in his masterpiece *Leviathan* (1651), called money 'the blood of the commonwealth'. Later, John Locke, in the *Second Treatise of Government*, offered quite unwittingly a theoretical justification of agrarian capitalism and its process of enclosure. Out of long personal experience including his leading role in the English colonization of Ireland and the redistribution of Irish lands, William Petty formulated a labour theory of value and is widely credited with fathering the science of political economy. The world was shortly given the shattering paradox of 'Private Vices, Publick Benefits' by Bernard de Mandeville in *Fable of the Bees* (1723). All these symbolic and suggestive occurrences reached a climax in 1776 with Adam Smith's publication of his great classic, *The Wealth of Nations*.

2

I turn now to Adam Smith (1723–90), and include some remarks about his fellow Scot, David Hume (1711–76), and Irish-born Edmund Burke (1729–97). These three friends formed a scintillating trinity of contemporary British thinkers of the Enlightenment. Smith was deeply indebted intellectually to Hume, and Burke owed much of his mature economic outlook to Smith. The differences and similarities of the economic ideas of the three are worth noting, if only in passing.

David Hume believed that avarice is embedded in human nature because of our inherent self-love and vanity, forcing us, whenever possible, to increase our pleasure and decrease our pain. He penned an early essay, of 1741, on avarice. Neither Hume nor his close friend Adam Smith, however, thought that humans are solely and simply by nature creatures of avarice and ambition. Avarice by itself, if unchecked, is a destructive force spelling the ruin of society. Fortunately, humans are also naturally endowed with 'sympathy' or fellow-feeling and with 'benevolence'. Both of these natural traits serve to counter-balance socially divisive avarice, binding us together instead of separating us. For Hume, avarice tends to vary with the changing historical situation, developing and increasing over the three historical stages of mankind, his categories being hunting–fishing, agriculture and commerce. Property and the passion for increasing possessions arise because of avarice. Without avarice there would be no property, nor would there be government, the institution devised by humans to protect and secure property. Above all else, commercial society, the latest stage of human evolution, according to Hume, the one in which he and his western European contemporaries were living, is animated by avarice. The dynamic of the economic system of commercial society is greed for property, possessions and profit.

Hume was far too fond of his own commercial society and aware of its advantages as against previous stages of history to give anything more than an ambiguous verdict on its merits. He was certainly aware of its defects, stemming from the fact that greed for gain was at the heart of its energy, industry and drive. Yet he definitely believed that the blooming of the arts and sciences, the expansion of knowledge, and the growth of luxury, all of which bring pleasure to many and which he likewise cherished, depend ultimately on the impetus of avarice. Nevertheless, he seems hesitant to deliver a judgment on the eventual outcome of this paradoxical historical process. But Adam Smith's humane and penetrating analysis pushed Hume's reservations and hesitations to their limit, although both Scottish thinkers rejected the hoary convention that the domination of avarice spelled inevitable social disintegration. In some sense, both were following the trail blazed by Thomas Smith.

We should avoid accepting uncritically and without qualification the widely held opinion today that Adam Smith in his classic *Wealth of Nations* pioneered the free market, the minimal state and the industrial capitalist economy. A virtual mythology has grown up in recent years, distorting and over-simplifying much of what Smith actually said. Smith, as we shall see, had serious reservations about commercial society, going well beyond Hume's rather bland scepticism. Before examining Smith's views, it should be stressed that he (unlike Hume) very rarely employed the words 'avarice' and 'avidity' in his classic. His preference was for 'interest' by itself or in conjunction with 'public', 'private' and 'self', and other nouns like 'profit', 'gain' and 'advantage'. Thus really begins the replacement in our vocabulary of the value-laden and malignant 'avarice' by more neutral and more benign terms which cause little offence, thus avoiding the moral opprobrium previously associated with and still attached to 'avarice'. In my treatment of Smith, however, I have taken the liberty of using 'avarice' in examining his ideas, without, I think, invalidating their meaning.

Broadly speaking, Smith takes over and expands much of Hume's approach to history. A convenient place to begin our brief assessment is Smith's well-known four-stage conception of history, based on the predominant mode of economic subsistence: hunting, pastoral, agricultural and commercial. In the distant past, life became more complex as the population grew and human needs multiplied; government was established to protect private property; property differentials increased in a pre-civil condition. The primary purpose of government was to protect the rich against the poor, each historical stage producing its own hierarchy of social relations and supporting institutions.

Smith opines, in his *Theory of Moral Sentiments* (1759), that the quest for wealth and power, moved by avarice and ambition, originates in the 'self-love' and 'vanity' of individuals desirous of displaying their prowess and success before others. Avarice, as previously noted, is in his view counter-balanced in the human make-up by 'benevolence' and 'sympathy'. Without them, society would degenerate into a free-for-all, but the ever present social danger is that they might be overwhelmed by avarice. He agrees with Hume that in early historical stages, life was simple, population sparse, and human needs few. Avarice and ambition were then in abeyance, not fomenting strife among people.

But in the commercial stage, avarice and ambition came to the fore. Avarice became the generator of economic life. The *Theory of Moral Sentiments* refers to the 'natural selfishness and rapacity of the rich' with 'their own vain and insatiable desires'. Smith's antipathy to the greed of the affluent also punctuates the *Wealth of Nations* with angry remarks about self-seeking merchants and manufacturers at the core of the commercial economy. He castigates them for their 'impertinent jealousy', 'mean rapacity' and 'monopolising spirit'. Merchants and manufacturers, he underscores, 'neither are, or ought to be the rulers of mankind'. Their 'interested sophistry has confounded the common sense of mankind'.

To understand Smith's anger with merchants and manufacturers in his own commercial society, one must always keep in mind several fundamental axioms of his political economy in the *Wealth of Nations*. First, agriculture is the foundation of an advanced commercial economy. Or, as he puts it in a more general way, land is 'by far the greatest, the most important, and the most durable part of the wealth of any extensive country'. Another principle is that the sole objective of all economic production is consumption. The interests of consumers must always take priority over those of producers. Furthermore, the interest of the vast majority is to be able to buy what they wish at the lowest price. Finally, the chief purpose of state and government in commercial society is the prosperity of everyone, not just a few.

The vexing problem with merchants and manufacturers in commercial Britain, Smith argues, is their persistent, overriding investment in movable capital, in less durable, less stable and in the long run less productive spheres than land. Their investments depend upon their perception of where profit is the highest in the short term. Again, because their greed for profit leads them to invest for the greatest immediate gain, their main aim is to produce their commodities at the lowest costs and sell them to consumers at the highest prices. Not the least of the reasons for Smith's ill-concealed ire with merchants and manufacturers is their continual monopolizing efforts. In order to increase profits by eliminating competition they perpetually try to monopolize domestic production, and prevent the influx of foreign goods that might undercut the prices of their own commodities. These tendencies to control the home market, thereby driving up prices and swelling their profits, and to restrict free trade, clearly negate the basic tenets of Smith's political economy. Essentially, he explicitly affirms, the interests of merchants and manufacturers conflict with the public interest as he defines it. Their interest always differs from the public interest, is sometimes diametrically opposed to it, and they have often 'deceived and oppressed' the public on this matter. He warns us to be wary of any commercial regulation proposed by merchants and manufacturers, which may in reality disguise their own narrow interests in the name of the public interest.

How then does Smith reconcile such an unflattering portrayal of the motivation of merchants and manufacturers with his memorable conception of the 'invisible hand', the mechanism ensuring that as long as individuals pursue their own interests without government interference, the result will be in the public interest? At the same time he believes that the hallmark of the successful commercial society is a vibrant and vigorous order of merchants and manufacturers, whose wealth and power are ever growing, but whose interest is at odds with, and sometimes even directly against, the public interest. The apparent contradiction can be resolved if a vital and neglected point made by Smith is not overlooked. He stipulates that only under specific conditions does the 'invisible hand' properly function to harmonize private interest with the public interest.

The absolutely necessary condition for the operation of the 'invisible hand' (mentioned only once in *Wealth of Nations* and once in *Theory of Moral Sentiments*) is what he calls the 'natural system of perfect liberty and justice'. Without this crucial condition the 'invisible hand' is simply inoperable. What then is the 'natural system', so necessary for the functioning of the 'invisible hand'? The key is government, and the positive action of government. In commercial society government must make and rigorously enforce laws freeing private economic activity from any interference, securing competition, preventing monopoly, forwarding free trade, and at the same time safeguarding private property, upholding contracts, compelling the payment of debts, and prohibiting any individual from unjustly infringing upon the activity of any other individual. Government must also build and maintain at public expense extensive public works – roads, canals, harbours – that will facilitate the movement of persons, goods and raw materials. A final and all-important role of government in creating a 'natural system' to underwrite the 'invisible hand' is its subsidizing of public institutions like universities and parish schools for the education of youth of every class. All of this must be accomplished by government with an eye to the public interest, the prosperity and happiness not just of a small minority but of all citizens, and, of course, the priority of consumption over production. Government, therefore, quite clearly from Smith's standpoint, has an essential interventionist function in initiating and fostering the social and political environment required for the successful operation of the 'invisible hand'. Smith unswervingly prescribes a state that will take positive action in this manner, intervening whenever necessary to activate the 'invisible hand'.

Whom, then, is Smith to rely upon for instituting and maintaining the 'natural system of perfect liberty and justice'? Who is to counter the greed and narrow self-interest of merchants and manufacturers? Who will be the custodians of the public interest, rationally and moderately steering the ship of state in advanced commercial society?

Because Smith profoundly distrusted merchants and manufacturers, and since he was by no stretch of the imagination inclined to democracy, his obvious choice for the critical role of governance is the agrarian class of landlords and prosperous farmers. Smith was exceedingly fond of rural life and favoured countrymen over townsmen. He was deeply distressed by the awful plight of urban workers in commercial society, those subject to the mindless and physically debilitating drudgery of the onerous routine of manufacture. He was greatly impressed by the endeavours of landlords and farmers who sought to increase production and hence their profits by means of agricultural improvement. He urges merchants and manufacturers to invest in landed property and its improvement. Agrarian capitalists (obviously unknown to him by that term) and other agriculturists are for Smith the vital pulse and safeguard of a thriving commercial society.

Since land and agriculture are the mainstay of commercial society, Smith exalts the class of landlords and well-to-do farmers as a kind of 'natural aristocracy' who should assume the leading part in the conduct of public affairs. A number of telling reasons is given for his choice. Country gentlemen and farmers are 'least subject to the wretched spirit of monopoly'. Instead, they promote the cultivation of their neighbours' farms and estates, and, living dispersed in the countryside, are much less prone to combine than are merchants and manufacturers. Most significant is his belief that the landed class better reflects the public interest than any of the other social orders because their capital investment is of a permanent and durable nature, rooted in their own country. This is in pronounced contrast to the capital investments of merchants and manufacturers who are likely to invest anywhere in the world, wherever the lure of immediate gain is the most seductive. Capital investments in land, moreover, are always a matter of public record, available to any interested person, whereas those of merchants and manufacturers are invariably secret, concealed from public inspection.

Smith was convinced, nevertheless, that greed for profit and possessions and ambition for power and office are absolutely indispensable to the development of civilized life as he knew it. Fundamental to the economic system of commercial society, of course, is avarice. Thus he breaks with the millennia-long condemnation of avarice as subversive of social and political unity, following in the wake of Thomas Smith. And not so far removed from Thomas Smith's artificial harmony of interests is Adam Smith's own notion of the 'invisible hand' and the natural harmony of interests. This is due to the latter's conviction that an interventionist government is basic to the shaping and conservation of the conditions most favourable to the realization of that natural harmony.

The admiration for a well-ordered and prospering commercial society that Smith expresses in the *Wealth of Nations* is, however, qualified by serious doubts, more pronounced and clearly defined than those of Hume. Some of these reservations in the *Wealth of Nations*, and in a new chapter added in the year of Smith's death to the 1790 edition of the earlier *Theory of Moral Sentiments*, almost seem to revert to the traditional criticism of avarice. In the *Wealth of Nations*, as we have seen, he never tires of chastizing the avaricious behaviour of merchants and manufacturers, the chief builders of commercial society, who threaten and undermine the public interest and must be controlled by the natural aristocracy of landlords and affluent farmers. In addition, his scepticism about commercial society is reflected in his humane anxiety over the debilitating lives of manufacturing labourers.

Some of these criticisms of avarice and its consequences for commercial society are even more evident in *Theory of Moral Sentiments*. There, in the first edition of 1759, he avers that greed and the accumulation of wealth and possessions are empty personal gratification. They are simply delusory if our major aim in life is bodily and mental well-being, for they constitute a great deception that 'keeps in motion the industry of mankind', thus accounting for most of the outstanding characteristics of civilized life.

Smith's final judgment on the great deception fashioning and permeating commercial society is found in the new chapter added to the seventh edition of the book just before his death. The new chapter is entitled: 'Of the corruption of our moral sentiments, which is occasioned by this disposition to admire the rich and the great and to despise or neglect persons of poor and mean condition'. Here, Smith takes to task the obsessive hold exercised by avarice and ambition over all members of society, especially among the poor majority. Everyone seems to be mesmerized by admiration and respect for the behaviour of the wealthy and powerful, and feverishly attempts to imitate them. While in most vocations, Smith states, success normally rests on ability, prudence, justice, firmness and temperance, this is not so among the eminent figures of commercial society, where success and preferment depend 'upon the fanciful and foolish favour of ignorant, presumptuous and proud superiors; flattery and falsehood too often prevail over merit and abilities'. The fundamental problem perceived by Smith is that these questionable figures become the role models for the rest of the population. In a society devoted to the acquisition of wealth and the perpetual chase after profits and possessions, when avarice becomes the leading motive in the lives of people, and poverty is despised and the poor are neglected, moral corruption spreads so rapidly and on such a colossal scale, penetrating every nook and cranny, that the inevitable result is social disintegration. Or such seems to be the implication of Smith's serious worries. Whether or not a flourishing commercial society generates the seeds of its own destruction because of its foundation on the dynamic of avarice is a crucial question that he leaves unanswered.

Now, in conclusion, a brief comment is required on Burke and subsequent developments. Like Smith, Burke holds that a natural aristocracy of the landed class should be a moderating and directing influence in governing commercial society. For the historical record, Burke, not Smith, seems to be the first British thinker to employ the word 'capitalist', two years before his friend Arthur Young did in *Travels in France* (1792). Significantly, the expression 'landed capitalist' occurs in Burke's *Reflections on the French Revolution* (1790). Unlike Smith, Burke does not hesitate to use 'avarice', assigning to it an absolutely fundamental part in civilized society. Reminiscent of Thomas Smith is Burke's remark of 1796–97 that

> it is for the statesman to employ it [avarice] as he finds it, with all its concomitant excellencies on its head. It is his part, in this case, as in all other cases, where he is to make use of the general energies of Nature, to take them as he finds them.

From Burke's vantage point, the duty of the natural aristocracy is to manipulate avarice for the nation's welfare.

Burke's sole work devoted to the economy is the short *Thoughts and Details of Scarcity* (1795), which obviously owed a great deal to Adam Smith. It was written in passionate opposition to the decision of the Speenhamland justices in Berkshire (Burke had acquired a 600-acre estate in adjoining Buckinghamshire) to provide subsidies for farm labourers who had fallen on hard times and were living below the subsistence level. Fearing that the Speenhamland ruling might become national policy, Burke argues for a market free from all government intervention.

In general, Burke concentrates on the agrarian sector, for as he stipulates, following Adam Smith, 'the agriculture of the kingdom [is] the first of all its concerns, and the foundation of all its prosperity'. Farmers' profits, he contends, are derived from the surplus created by farm labourers. If market demand for farmers' produce declines, in order to maintain their profits, wages paid by them to their workers must fall proportionately. Each individual envies the prosperity of every other. 'But if the farmer is naturally avaricious', Burke comments, referring to good times for agriculture, 'why so much the better: the more he desires to increase his gains, the more interested is he in the good conditions of these upon whose labour his gains must principally depend'. When times are bad, however, his workers must accept their lot, a necessary decline in their wages, proportionate to the fall in demand for their labour. The economic laws of supply and demand, Burke insists, must be allowed to take their course, without any external interference, because they are the 'laws of nature' that in turn are the 'laws of God'. In the long run 'Divine Providence' will prevent the undue hardship and suffering of the workers. Government should have a minimal function, refraining from intervening in the economy. Nature must be allowed to take its course. The harmony of interests over the long term arising from 'Divine Providence' is Burke's substitute for Smith's 'invisible hand', without the latter's qualification of the requisite conditions for its operation created by an interventionist state. One can only draw the rather startling conclusion that in Burke's scheme of things avarice is divinely ordained and programmed, the indispensable basis of the civilized social order. Notably missing also from his political economy is Smith's deep and abiding compassion for the plight of the working majority, his humane anxiety over the corruption of commercial society, and his apparent scepticism as to the possible future of such a society.

After Burke, the value-laden 'avarice' virtually disappears from the economic, social and political vocabulary. For instance, in the next century, in the writings of a host of economic thinkers like Malthus,

Ricardo, Gay, McCulloch, Bentham and J.S. Mill, the previous, morally stigmatized 'avarice' seems to be all but replaced by the neutral, non-pejorative 'interest', 'self-interest', 'profit' and so on. While these terms were commonly employed before, during the previous three centuries 'avarice', as we have seen, was still a subject of discussion. From the nineteenth century to the present, 'interest', not 'avarice', is taken for granted as the generator of the economy and the very foundation of the interdependence of individuals, and consequently of social unity. Avarice is now respectably clothed so as to disguise what was long deemed to be one of the worst characteristics of human behaviour and a dire threat to social order. 'Avarice', well-tailored and hidden behind the concept of 'interest', far from being thought of as aberrant human behaviour is now the normal and legitimate way of things.

A broad avenue had thus been opened for the unimpeded passage and accelerating speed of the capitalist mentality. In our own age of rampant consumerism, we are ignorant of avarice and its social perils, only cognizant of the integrity of interest and self-interest. Wealth has become the much sought-after goal, the cherished ideal of many people living in advanced capitalist society. Indeed, one of the great delusions of the times is that capitalism offers an equal opportunity to all for the attainment of money and possessions. Avarice, by any other name, is now a benign good, the vital pulse of the capitalist mentality moving people to support and justify the capitalist organization of society. Without the universal and unreflective faith in the merits of the hidden hand of interest and self-interest, capitalism would soon lose the momentum and energy that catapulted it to world domination. Perhaps it is not too late to revive and renew some of the illuminating and thought-provoking scepticism not only of Adam Smith but also of Karl Marx. The paramount question to ask in our self-analysis is relatively simple and straightforward. Can a society, like advanced capitalist America, without imminent or serious threat to its survival, hold together and avoid decay, if its most acclaimed and universally lauded ideal is the unbridled pursuit of individual acquisition? Can a society whose fundamental premise is uninhibited material self-advancement possibly cohere, or must it be engulfed at some time in the future by a deluge of its own making? Does advanced capitalist society contain by its very essence the seeds of self-destruction?

DEMOCRACY DEFANGED AND TRANSFIGURED

Besides the transformation in attitude to avarice, another gradual and related change in outlook was also crucial in shaping our contemporary capitalist mentality. This was the eventual metamorphosis of a commonly held view of democracy (connected with the problem of social unity), giving it a wholly new dimension and meaning. The link between the two inversions of values is, of course, capitalism, whose spokesmen seem highly adept in fashioning novel conceptual distortions to serve its ideological purposes. This chapter will treat the second momentous transmutation of values, beginning with some thoughts about an ancient idea of social change and about the origin of the principle of sovereignty, before focusing on the notion of democracy itself.

1

Ancient Greek and Roman thinkers worked out a fairly comprehen-sive and coherent conception of what we might label social change. Among them was the military commander and statesman, Sallust (*c.* 86–36 BC). He effectively launched Roman historiography with two extant monographs, and a history of the years 78–67 BC, most of which has been lost. In them he articulates a widely accepted counsel of prudence: fear of an external enemy promotes unity within the state. His 'theorem' was the conclusion of studying the Roman past in order to discover a causal explanation for the social discord and moral degeneration of his own day. The major reason for the decay, he contends, lay in the Roman destruction of its arch-enemy Carthage in 146 BC. Prior to this definitive victory, social and political harmony was maintained and serious internal conflict avoided because of the fear instilled in the Roman people by their 200-year-long struggle (interspersed by periods of peace) against their formidable Punic adversary.

After 146 BC no threats to Roman survival and hegemony remained in the Mediterranean world. Extended peace and increasing pros-perity – the spoils of victory from the ever expanding empire, according to Sallust – unleashed in Romans the lust for wealth, luxury and power. Greed for riches and possessions disrupted the previous generally prevailing social and political solidarity. No longer dedi-cating themselves, as they had in the past, to honour, integrity, the pursuit of laudable ambition, and the veneration of the gods, Sallust tells us, Romans were now driven by their apparently insatiable appetites into licentious behaviour and constant internecine strife. Civil turmoil ruled the day. Youths were corrupted and poverty was considered a disgrace. Caught up in a frenetic chase after money and profits, Romans 'set a price on everything'. The fall of Carthage removed the major obstacle to internal contention, resulting in civil war and moral decline. Or such was the opinion of Sallust, whose words on the subject, although little known today, were avidly read by countless future generations.

Sallust's historical interpretation was later reinforced by the legendary story about Marcus Cato the Elder and Nasica Corculum, told by the Greek historian Posidonius, and immortalized in Plutarch's famous version. In it, we are informed that Cato, the doughty elder statesman of the republic, distraught about the burgeoning military might of an increasingly prospering Carthage during a prolonged lull in hostilities between the two foes before 146 BC, demanded its immediate destruction. Apparently obsessed by the thought of once and for ever ending the Punic threat, he reportedly punctuated his every speech in the Senate with the battlecry: 'Delenda est Carthago [Carthage must be destroyed]'. A fellow senator, Nasica, cousin of the great Scipio Africanus Major, who finally vanquished Carthage in 146 BC, argued the contrary. Fear of Carthage, he emphasized in opposition to Cato, was an absolutely necessary constraint on the Roman people. The wisdom of his alternative to Cato's proposal, Nasica maintained, was based on the fact that the Carthaginians were 'too weak to overcome the Romans, and too great to be despised by them'.

Sallust's theorem was probably of military provenance, originating in the tactical shrewdness of the seasoned commander. With the cessation of hostilities and a period of prolonged peace, an army commander would more than likely have some difficulty in preserving the discipline, morale and harmony of his troops. This fracturing solidarity would soon be corrected when their survival was once again threatened by renewed confrontation with an enemy. Long before Sallust the theorem was readily translatable into a prudential axiom of government, no doubt reflecting the origins of the state in an armed camp engaging in military raids against the perpetual incursions of hostile foes. So Aristotle recommended that in the absence of an actual enemy, fear of which assured the order of the state because of the citizens' concern for their survival, the astute statesman should deliberately fabricate an external threat to serve that very purpose. And centuries after Sallust, Machiavelli's ideas about military and civil unity are infused with this theorem. Later in the sixteenth century the illustrious Jean Bodin even observes that God permits wars and hatred among nations in order to maintain and strengthen the virtue of their citizens, not solely to punish his errant children for their transgressions.

The perspective of Sallust and other ancient and early modern thinkers is closely associated with a typically *pre-capitalist* model of the state. Since time immemorial the state was in theory and practice a 'guild of warriors' – to use Max Weber's felicitous term – of citizens, however defined, capable of bearing arms in defence of the homeland. Such a characterization appears to be applicable to ancient Greece, republican Rome, mediaeval kingdoms and Renaissance city-states. Interstate warfare and struggle were endemic, the normal situation rather than the exception. As long as the threat of an external foe existed, avarice was kept in check and the internal unity of the state secured. Fear of a foreign enemy, real or imagined, tightly knit together the social fabric of the state, aided by the power of punishment exercised by commanders and rulers for any breach of law and order.

Over the centuries this outlook underwent an interesting transposition when states were no longer threatened with instant annihilation and warfare became less frequent, although peace among nations was still far from being normal. Under such relatively pacific circumstances, the state's internal unity could no longer depend so much on fear of a foreign enemy. In those shifting conditions, the idea gradually evolved that fear of an external enemy might be internalized and domesticated. This insight seems to have been translated into the early modern concept of sovereignty, most notably constructed by Jean Bodin and Thomas Hobbes.

Sovereignty, conceived by them and others, is the supreme and indivisible law-making power possessed by an individual or institution within the state. The sovereign enforces law through a monopoly of coercive force, the ultimate sanction for a legal violation being the power of life and death over all citizens. Sovereignty in principle and practice became the generally accepted solution to the problems of social unity and of controlling avarice, and the defining mark of the state. The sovereign in effect is the supreme commander of the army of citizens and, in the absence of an external threat to survival, keeps them in order by means of coercion and the threat of coercion. The sovereign is the guarantor of social harmony and manager of the state's welfare, preventing avarice and self-seeking from jeopardizing civil order. Thus described, the concept of sovereignty is basically pre-capitalist in origins, nevertheless continuing to be a cherished and valuable idea throughout the capitalist era to the present, a central concept of both national and international law. With the development of English capitalism, however, as we have seen, from the standpoint of social unity, the principle of sovereignty was soon supplemented, but by no means replaced, by the innovative perception that economic interdependence brought about by the interplay of interest and self-interest in the pursuit of profit was vital to social solidarity.

2

The ancient Athenians engaged in an unprecedented democratic experiment which lasted for nearly two hundred years in the sixth and fifth centuries BC. Many future generations were to consider this to be the world's first democracy, indeed the archetype of democracy, traditionally classified as one of the three major types of government: the rule of one, the few and the many, i.e. monarchy, oligarchy and democracy. Athens may have been the first democracy in human history, but from our standpoint at the beginning of the twenty-first century it suffered from serious flaws. Women were excluded from any political role, as were resident aliens and a large slave population. Nevertheless, it was unique for its time and for centuries to come in that every male citizen (country as well as city dwellers) regardless of family, upbringing, property and income was eligible for full political participation and office holding. Democracy, to use Aristotle's description, was the 'rule of the poor'. This in itself, despite the serious blemishes, was a truly revolutionary idea. We should, of course, not be carried away by this idea of people's power, for in practice the affluent, leisured minority tended to dominate Athenian politics, Pericles being the best-known example. The disparity, however, between the wealth of the rich and the poor was by our own standards not excessive.

Procedurally, Athenian democracy entailed direct rule by all male citizens. This meant debate and voting by show of hands (not by secret ballot, a Roman innovation) in the 'sovereign' assembly on measures to be adopted, the choice by lot of leading officials, and participation in the gigantic popular juries. Payment for assembly attendance was made, so that poor citizens would not endure economic hardship because of absence from work. In time of danger, all citizens were expected to bear arms in the land or sea forces. Substantially, democracy for Athenians was intimately related to the rule of law and equality before the law, *isonomia*, and with immunity from the arbitrary will of others, *eleutheria*. Democracy to the Athenian significantly implied compassion for the weak and unfortunate.

Little evidence has survived about the ideas of the great contemporary champions of Athenian democracy, in marked contrast to
the extant and extensive criticisms made by its opponents. Still sur-
viving are Pericles' great 'Funeral Oration', recorded by Thucydides,
fragments of Protagoras' many writings, Plato's dialogue *Protogoras*,
some remarks of the great atomist Democritus, and passing thoughts
in the voluminous orations of Demosthenes. They all seem to confirm
the existence of a vibrant consensual politics of common sense and
pragmatism and the priority given to the rule of law, freedom and
equality in the self-government of the citizen body. During those two
centuries of democracy, disparities of income among citizens were not
exceptionally large, nor were there any enormous concentrations of
economic power. With some exceptions, Athens could be called a
relatively egalitarian society of neither the very rich nor the very poor,
a far cry from the situation in the late Roman republic and empire.

The copious words of condemnation of the much better-known
foes and critics of Athenian democracy – reading like an intellectual
Who's Who of antiquity, including Socrates, Plato, Thucydides,
Xenophon, Isocrates, Aristotle, Polybius, Cicero, Seneca – have,
unlike the advocates of democracy, survived and profoundly influ-
enced the way the Athenian experiment has been viewed over the
centuries. The verdict has been almost entirely negative, until very
recently. The vilification of Athenian democracy and democracy in
general is commonly linked with a somewhat nebulous conception of
social change and corruption. Sallust, as previously noted, offers less a
theory of social corruption than one of moral decay. Fearful of the
unleashing of avarice and its subversion of social unity, phenomena in
the Rome of his day, he maintains that such degeneration can be
blocked by the presence of an external enemy. Apart from his 'theorem' and insight about the negative impact of widespread avarice on
social cohesion, he suggests or implies points stressed in more detail

by the other vociferous critics of democracy in classical antiquity. They express a common upper-class disdain for the lower classes, an obsessive fear of democracy and, related to this fear, a distinctive conception of social corruption and social health in which the dreaded rise of avarice plays a prominent part.

Their reasoning is something like the following. Democracy, or the direct rule of the people, creates conditions conducive to the growth of social corruption and moral decay. Under democracy, the poor lower classes in their domination of the state free themselves from the control of their social betters. Members of the populace contend with each other and their former social superiors for money, possessions, power and status. Avarice and ambition pit citizen against citizen in a mêlée of self-advancement, destroying all sense of the common good. Democracy is soon transmuted into 'mob rule'. Amidst the mounting strife and corruption, the restoration of civil order is usually promised by an attractive popular figure, sometimes from the upper classes. After he has established himself as a tribune of the people and has consolidated his position, he eventually seizes state power, becoming a full-blown tyrant.

Much of this kind of opposition to democracy and fear of its consequences was motivated by the critics' upper-class snobbery and dread of the 'common herd', *hoi polloi*, who earned their livelihood in banausic labour and trade. When confined to the upper classes, avarice and profit-seeking (within limits), or so the anti-democratic critics seemed to believe, did not really threaten social unity. In a democracy, however, once the people were freed from subjection to the upper classes, their unbridled pursuit of riches and possessions would soon become socially divisive and menace the state. If tinkers and tailors, shopkeepers and manual workers achieved power in a democracy, their victory would be catastrophic, spelling the rapid demise of the previous peaceful and refined life of the well-to-do.

These views comprise, in essence, a doctrine of social corruption with its causally interrelated set of ideas about democracy, avarice, disunity and tyranny, a doctrine found in varying degrees and emphases in most thinkers from Plato to Machiavelli. As an antidote to this ever threatening danger, the critics of democracy have a vision of 'social health' to be achieved by a specific structuring of the state. In sum, they stipulate a state of distinctive social rankings under the rule of law, ultimately dominated by the affluent propertied classes. This arrangement would be based upon a 'mixed constitution' combining the rule of one, the few and the many; that is, a medley of monarchical, oligarchic and democratic traits. A system of checks and balances would be institutionalized, thereby impeding the threat of tyranny from both above and below, from both one-man rule and democracy. In this governmental scheme, the people are given some minimal role and voice, while never being able to control the state. Through education, broadly construed, and the good example of the socially superior propertied classes, the animating ideal of the social health to be established by the 'mixed constitution' would be the common good, as defined and implemented by the dominant propertied classes, instead of avarice and the accumulation of riches endemic to democracy.

3

From classical antiquity to the nineteenth century, democracy has been the most widely criticized form of government among social theorists and commentators. Most of the opponents of democracy, nevertheless, clearly recognized that it was not the only source of tyranny. Monarchy, without meticulously circumscribed powers and constant vigilance and oversight, could easily deteriorate into tyrannical and oppressive rule. Some of those haunted by what they thought to be the potentiality for tyranny in both democracy and monarchy became ardent republicans, advocating some version of the mixed constitution.

This seems to have been true of the constitutional fathers of the newly founded United States of America. The written constitution they designed and instituted embodied a governmental system enshrining the rule of law, the separation of powers with institutional checks and balances, a bicameral Congress of Senate and House of Representatives, only the latter being popularly elected; indirect election of the president and senators; an independent federal judiciary, appointed by the president and confirmed by the Senate; the federal/state division of powers, an elaborate amending process involving Congress and the states, and a Bill of Rights in the form of the first ten amendments. This was clearly not a democracy in any traditional sense, and was not intended to be by the founding fathers. The constitution was an ingenious and elaborate experiment in preventing tyranny by one, the few or the many, a variation of the time-hallowed 'mixture' with its goal of social health, the avoidance of civil corruption, and the safeguarding of the propertied classes. The constitutional limitations on the popular role in government would alone disqualify the fledging United States from being called a democracy, not to mention the property qualifications for voting imposed at the beginning by most states in the union.

Some lone voices – like Gerrard Winstanley in mid-seventeenth-century England and the Anglo-American Tom Paine at the end of the eighteenth century – vigorously espoused and defended democracy, but the French Revolution further fuelled the upper classes' terror of the great beast. Not until the nineteenth and twentieth centuries did democracy begin to shed its shroud of condemnation and vilification. Numerous factors contributed to the change of attitude. Among them the most significant was probably the industrialization of Great Britain, to be followed by western Europe and the United States. A soaring urban population and declining demographic dispersal in rural areas brought into close proximity countless numbers of people who suffered the appalling human abuses of early industrialization. The result of their strengthening protests against what they were being subjected to produced the trades union and socialist movements with their cries for social justice and the end of exploitation. The French Revolution may have frightened the upper classes, but by its radical actions and calls for liberty, equality and fraternity it fired the mounting protests of workers elsewhere and inspired their organizational efforts. The gradual democratization of the US constitution was both cause and effect, helping to contribute to the change of attitude. Eventually in the twentieth century democracy was given the seal of approval and was highly praised as a laudable political goal. Because of immense populations scattered over vast territories, the idea of democracy as direct rule of the people proved highly impracticable for the contemporary state. Democracy in the modern world, as Tom Paine long ago argued, could only be based on representation, on duly elected representatives of the people.

Democracy can be defined both procedurally and substantively, one definition focusing on individual liberty, the other on a broad social equality. Today 'democracy' is defined almost exclusively in procedural terms: government by representatives of the people chosen in periodic free elections. All citizens are entitled to the franchise regardless of sex, property, race, colour or religion. So defined, democratic government also signifies the rule of law, some constitutional structure of checks and balances, competing political parties, and guaranteed rights of the person, property, speech, assembly and religion. This definition is most typical of 'liberal democracies'. Little is said about how representative of the people their chosen representatives must be. In some countries (not the United States) fines are imposed on citizens for failure to cast their votes. Generally speaking, a deep distrust of 'majority rule' and of any direct role of the people in government still persists. The substantive question of social equality is seldom addressed. Can true democracy possibly exist in any society of staggering and skyrocketing disparities of wealth, income and property; where riches are increasingly concentrated in the hands of a growing minority, with no let-up in sight, and where only the wealthy can afford to stand for election? Even fewer are concerned with democracy in the workplace. Can there be any real democracy where the vast working majority are ever more subjected to authoritarian regimes in their factories, workshops and offices?

These problems have received some attention in the past from social democrats, and especially from democratic socialists. Now that socialism is in decline, however, the formal procedural aspects of democracy appear to have won the day, and less and less emphasis is being given to the critical substantive issues. 'Democracy' today seems to have become little more than a convenient, self-serving slogan applicable to any state – except the most obviously dictatorial and repressive regimes – that has a written constitution, a façade of representative government, and pays lip-service to democratic principles and the rule of law. By these criteria Peru, Mexico, Malaysia, Pakistan, Russia and the Baltic states are all democratic.

One fascinating exception to the marked lack of interest in the substantive definition of democracy (at least as understood in the past) is rapidly coming to the fore. This is the growing tendency to associate democracy with capitalism and the 'free market', even sometimes to the extent of identifying them. Although they are not usually equated, democracy is often said to imply capitalism, and capitalism in turn is conceived of as implying democracy, at best a rather far-fetched distortion of the historical record. For democracy and capitalism make quite strange bedfellows with very little in common, analytically and historically.

In fact, contrary to growing opinion, democracy and capitalism are polar opposites. Capitalist business corporations, their offices and workplaces, are inherently authoritarian, far removed from democratic procedure and substance. A capitalist enterprise organized and operated in a genuinely democratic fashion is inconceivable. Despite the fact that the Internet has rendered possible closer co-operation between comparable echelons of different corporations for the fruitful exchange and discussion of ideas and strategies, hierarchy and authority are still the functional operating procedures within a single enterprise. Commands flow from the top downwards in the typical capitalist concern, to be executed by those in the lower levels of the pyramid of power, to be carried out without question or deviation, although management often encourages debate and input from its subordinates to help in reaching a final decision. The authoritarian essence of the capitalist firm is frequently glossed over by introducing and publicizing the slogans 'team activity' and 'team spirit'. But the notion of 'team' itself, entailing as it does co-operation and the subordination of individual interest, opinion and action to the harmony and efficiency of the working group, is essentially authoritarian, whether it is several horses pulling a wagon or a collection of football players. One has a driver and the other a captain and coach. The use of 'team' when applied to a capitalist enterprise is basically a public relations ploy or a sop to the employees themselves, camouflaging the authoritarian structure of the business, with the aim of cultivating the solidarity of the workforce and spurring them on to ever greater loyalty, co-operative endeavour and productivity.

In addition to the conceptual incongruity of juxtaposing democracy and capitalism, our own historical experience belies any very intimate connection between them. Indeed, on the contrary, from the historical standpoint the theory and practice of democracy preceded capitalism by at least two thousand years. Capitalism first appeared in undemocratic western European societies in the modern era, in Great Britain, then in France and Germany. The United States embarked on the capitalist course of development well before democracy in any meaningful sense had been attained. On the basis of its historical origins, one is tempted to say that an undemocratic, even author-itarian, social, political and cultural environment is the most favourable condition for the emergence of capitalism. Quite clearly capitalism and the idea of a free market first came to fruition in mid-nineteenth-century Britain, still undemocratic in many ways. From then to the present, capitalism has risen and flourished in a host of authoritarian societies at one time or another, including Germany, Italy, Singapore, Hong Kong, China, Brazil, Argentina, Chile, South Africa and Indonesia.

4

Our historical odyssey has so far concentrated on the absolutely amazing inversion of values that in their new form seem to be at the core of the capitalist mentality so necessary to the world triumph of advanced capitalism. Without the ideological underpinning of this mentality's new version of avarice and democracy, the system would be helpless. This revolutionary transformation, occurring over a long period, was of course a response to the accelerating growth of capitalism. First, the threat of avarice to social unity was ideologically changed into the very foundation of that unity, treated as a benign good instead of a malignant growth. Second, and lagging behind this miraculous shift, democracy, rather than being considered a danger to social unity by freeing avarice, also came to be regarded as a worthy goal and natural partner and helpmate of capitalism, if not identical with capitalism itself. Avarice, in the guise of interest and self-interest, is now perceived to be the very essence of capitalist society, its prime motor and the crucial basis of social solidarity and well-being. Democracy has at last been made respectable and legitimate. It is no longer a threat to social unity. Like the free play of avarice, once so excoriated, democracy in effect is thought to promote interest and self-interest, i.e. avarice in its new clothing, reinforcing and forwarding the capitalist dynamic.

'Democracy' has been accepted and eulogized rather late in the day, almost as an ideological afterthought, perhaps, among other reasons, to help rationalize and conceal capitalist authoritarian practice. In the early twenty-first century, 'democracy' has been reduced to little more than a slogan, an ideological sleight of hand masking the authoritarian nature of capitalist enterprise and expansion, and its domination of politics and government. Constant invocation of 'democracy' and its linkage with capitalism and the free market seem designed, albeit unconsciously, to render people more flexible and enthusiastic consumers of the vast and ever changing flow of commodities on whose constant and increasing sales capitalist business so depends. When so closely coupled with capitalism, democracy today in practice resembles nothing so much as Aristotle's conception of *timocracy*, political power in proportion to property holdings. In our contemporary democracies those with the greatest amounts of property exert infinitely more influence on vital political decisions than the ever growing propertyless majority. Affluent property holders, unlike ordinary citizens, have easy access to the corridors of power and an important part, completely disproportionate to their small numbers, in the shaping and implementation of public policy. Nor should we overlook the fact that democracy is often identified with constitutionalism and the rule of law, neither of which venerable concepts is in theory or practice necessarily related to democratic government.

Democracy in today's parlance has largely been legitimized because in a very significant way it has been made toothless. Far from Aristotle's meaning of 'rule of the poor', democracy has been transfigured by the ever tighter grip exerted by rich capitalists and their enterprises over government. Admittedly, they exercise control through the rule of law, but there seems to be one law for the wealthy and another for the poor. Emphasis given to its procedural aspects, important as they are, has obscured democracy's crucial substantive nature, discussion of which has all but disappeared from popular and learned disquisitions on democratic problems. A division of labour has consigned to capitalism a supreme economic function, and to its partner, democracy, a political function, thereby reducing the latter to being the minion of the former, a reflex of capitalism in the political arena. Democracy is increasingly little more than capitalism by other means. By jettisoning social equality, political equality and even equality before the law (the much vaunted characteristics of democratic procedures), democracy has been emasculated. For to date the rule of capitalism through the political instruments of democracy has in actual practice produced dire social and political inequalities and inequities, extremes in wealth and power without historical precedent. Moreover, can true democracy exist in a society in which people are so ill-informed about the urgent public issues at home and abroad? Can democracy truly exist when society has become a vast theatre for little more than the entertainment of citizens? Education in the broadest sense, not entertainment in the crudest sense, indeed education of a very high level, seems to be absolutely fundamental to a vigorous democracy. And what has happened to high levels of education in a society increasingly premised upon the 'dumbing down' of the intellect? Last but not least, what of the physical well-being and health of citizens? Can a democracy possibly thrive, engage citizens in its complex activities, and inspire their loyalty, when vast numbers are ill-nourished and ill-housed, often with little or no access to proper medical attention? These problems go to the very heart of democracy, analysed today almost entirely in terms of conformity to specific procedures and institutional arrangements without the existence of these absolutely necessary social conditions. No wonder that so many citizens in contemporary democracies display such apathy to politics and distrust of and contempt for politicians.

Democracy has at last been legitimized, only to become the mindless servant of authoritarian capitalism. This astounding development reflects the changing attitude towards avarice and social unity. The basic reason in both cases for the transmutation of values appears to be the rise and development of capitalism in modern times. Another related change of practical import occurs with the traditional concept of social corruption, in the past closely associated with democracy, avarice, civil disorder and tyranny. Social corruption in its original meaning is now no longer believed to be a social abnormality spelling the ruin of the state. The old social corruption has in some ways been transmuted into the normal circumstance of progressive democratic society, legitimized and institutionalized as the natural way of life. Yesterday's social corruption is today's social health.

Capitalism has turned the world of human relations and values upside down in the last four to five hundred years, something seldom appreciated by those with little or no historical understanding; unfortunately this means most people, even many of the better educated. Democratic society in the early twenty-first century suffers from collective amnesia. Most who lack a grasp of history fail to appreciate that capitalism legitimizes and institutionalizes greed for money and possessions, previously denounced by pagan and Christian moralists. Under the sway of an ever enlarging and advancing capitalism, opposition to avarice, social corruption and democracy has been transcended by a semantic sleight of hand. In shaping the capitalist mentality, they have ceased to be the frightening spectres of social catastrophe, to be avoided at all costs. Capitalism through the ideological justification and motor of the capitalist mentality has transformed what was once considered social illness into its polar opposite, social health, the natural condition of the body politic.

This perspective reached some kind of climax with Reaganism and Thatcherism (still revered by American Republicans and British Conservatives) and their influential postulate: 'society', or so we are constantly reminded, is little more than a collection of atomistic individuals, each competing with the others to increase profits and decrease monetary losses. Old social corruption is thus rendered respectable, transformed into 'civility', a state not of illness but of health, a condition of normality, conceived of as the impetus, the vigorous motor of capitalism and the people living and working in an advanced capitalist order. To the capitalist mentality, the threat of tyranny, once considered to be the inevitable result of the disarray of a corrupt society, is now an acceptable way of life under the protective shield of democracy. Paradoxically, the new standard of social health in practice masks the emergence of a new form of tyranny, the tyranny of advanced capitalism and capitalist culture, subjecting everyone – impoverished and prosperous, weak and powerful – to its insidious and all-pervasive regime; and most alarmingly, threatening to engulf the planet.

5

Has there been any value in these historical ruminations, or do they represent self-indulgence in antiquarianism of only marginal contemporary relevance? Perhaps they have alerted us to the fact that in the past when there has been a single omnipotent superpower without rival upon the world scene, it has been subject to decay and breakdown. When all imminent threats to the survival of that superpower have been removed, past sages have attributed its subsequent degeneration to the displacement of social co-operation and unity by an aggregation of sharply competing individuals, each pursuing self-interest to the detriment of the common good in a frenzied struggle for the acquisition of profits and possessions. The new phenomenon of capitalism, scarcely 150 years old as a developed system, is predicated by its very nature on greed and self-seeking, universalizing, institutionalizing and legitimizing them as 'interest' and 'self-interest' all in the guise of democracy. The capitalist mentality, arising from the growth and expansion of capitalism and becoming its ideological bulwark, justificatory and energizing, consists of an inversion of traditional beliefs and values, and exalts a well-disguised avarice, as well as transforming the theory and practice of democracy beyond all recognition.

These propositions resulting from historical reflection lead to several conclusions. Social decay in the long term may very well be inherent in capitalism because of its foundation in and dependence on the most socially divisive of human motives. This would seem to be more than a distinct possibility when the world's sole uncontested power is the capitalist behemoth of the United States. Then the process of decay may become so accelerated and universalized, and so hidden from view, that its way of life appears to be entirely normal and natural. Under such circumstances, the collapse of advanced capitalist society, perhaps triggered by a severe financial crash, ter-minating in a general breakdown, may only be a matter of time. The creative destruction at the very heart of capitalist activity could very well be terminated by a social collapse. At least the historical enquiries in the last two chapters may give us pause for thought about what the future holds.

4

THE NEW TYRANNY OF CAPITALISM

In the previous two chapters 'tyranny' has been frequently mentioned. This chapter will deal briefly with the concept by way of introducing Chapters 5 and 6, concerned with the impact of advanced capitalism on society and politics in the United States at the opening of the twenty-first century. So much has been said about contemporary capitalism, assessing both its virtues and vices, that it is very difficult to add anything novel or perceptive to the welter of words. But perhaps by approaching advanced capitalism somewhat differently, something enlightening can still be contributed. Therefore, in pursuing this objective and as a prelude to some details about American society and politics, I wish to treat very broadly the character of advanced capitalism under the rubric of tyranny, which I shall suggest has taken two major forms: *old tyranny* and *new tyranny*.

1

Old tyranny is fundamentally, though not exclusively, a political category. From this standpoint, tyranny has traditionally denoted the exercise of supreme political power within the state (and lesser formal organizations) solely by a single individual or group of individuals. Since the Greeks coined the word, its meaning has become more pejorative. As heads of state or chief executives, or quite often the persons of real power behind these rulers or, for that matter, any social institution (family, church, labour union, professional society, etc.), tyrants subject others to their will in a repressive, intolerant, unjust and sometimes cruel and even terroristic fashion. Tyrannical rulers of states typically exert their power and authority arbitrarily and without legal right, although they may very well begin as legal and rightfully chosen rulers. Obviously there are different degrees of tyranny. The type outlined here is the full-blown tyrant. Some are more 'liberal', as it were, less repressive and less inhumane in their behaviour. The whim of the full-blown tyrant is the 'law of the land'. A mockery is made of the rule of law. Unchecked and unaccountable to any other individual or institution, such a tyrant suppresses all political opposition and criticism of the regime. As social and political theorists throughout the ages have certainly recognized, some tyrants are popular figures, not ruling by fear alone. They are able to mobilize vast public support through their personal charisma and the striking panoply of ritual and ceremony with which they embellish their power, and by the dispensation of favours and funds, and the sponsoring of lavish public festivities.

Since the origins of the organized state some five millennia ago, tyranny has been a persistent and unalloyed plague in the world. It shows few signs of abating in the early twenty-first century, even after the appalling experience of fascism, Nazism and Stalinism. Tyrants have come and gone with variable frequency. Usually their rule has been relatively short, often ending in disaster for themselves and their supporters. Tyrannies constantly appear, only to disappear, frequently in the same states. Yet tyrants and would-be tyrants never seem to learn the lesson of history. Among its victims and opponents, tyranny breeds hatred, opposition and the resolve to end the wilful abuse of power by one means or another, sometimes only to replace it by another tyranny. And so the scourge of tyranny moves interminably on. It is an old and often repeated story.

During the twentieth century old tyranny in the particularly malignant form of totalitarianism appeared in fascist Italy, the Soviet Union, Nazi Germany, eastern Europe, imperial Japan, communist China, North Korea and, in varying degrees, Franco's Spain and Salazar's Portugal. As the term indicates, these totalitarian variations of old tyranny go well beyond supreme political control in their usurpation of power and authority over not only government but also society, economy and culture. Totalitarianism was total, opening windows into human souls. While relatively short-lived, totalitarianism produced some of the most brutal and terroristic regimes known to humankind. In the post-Second World War era, with the exception of totalitarianism in North Korea and in a much 'liberalized' form in China, other kinds of tyranny have proliferated: in Indonesia, Malaysia, Yugoslavia, Iraq, Syria, Saudi Arabia, Iran, Libya, Sudan, Nigeria and Haiti, to name a few at random. Military dictatorships, of course, have come and gone in Africa and Latin America.

Why today are we still constantly beset with the problem of tyranny? Why does tyranny persist, and why do so many become tyrants, only to be eliminated and replaced by other tyrants? A searching examination of these important questions is not necessary here, but a few observations may be in order. Are tyrants simply ignorant and small-minded with little or no knowledge of history and its dire lessons about the fate of those like them? While this is true of some, many tyrants are intelligent and educated. On the whole they are a very clever breed. Are tyrants more susceptible than other mortals to the proverbial weakness of human nature, succumbing more readily than others to the allure of absolute power and all it has to offer, at least in the short run? Long before Lord Acton, Plato argued that because of the inherent frailty of human nature, all power corrupts, and absolute power corrupts absolutely. Hence, in the *Laws* he stresses that all rulers should be circumscribed by a rigorous system of law and elaborate institutional checks. Or is it that a would-be tyrant, a principled person with the very best of intentions, for example with an agenda for governmental reform, is determined to see his project through to the end? Once in power, however, he soon realizes that all is not as straightforward and simple as previously anticipated, and clings to power, ever enlarging it out of desperation for his own survival and the security of his supporters. Or do specific circumstances explain the persistence of tyranny? Does the state in question have no history of limiting power, only a long record of the abuse of power? Under such circumstances, tyranny is virtually a way of life, institutionalized in the culture as a traditional mode of political behaviour. Displacing such a norm seems to be extremely difficult, if not impossible. In such states (and elsewhere) seizing power and exercising it tyrannically may be the surest way of amassing riches and possessions.

Whatever the reasons for the tenacious grip of tyranny on so much of the present and past political world, any satisfactory explanation of a concrete instance must be an extraordinarily complex one, possibly involving some of the factors outlined above and undoubtedly others as well. Suffice it to stress that our understanding of tyranny should not rest on a simplistic notion of the frailty of human nature, on a concept of original sin or innate human greed, or on human irrationality. Such notions do a grave injustice to what we know of human behaviour in its multifarious social contexts.

Historically, the scourge of tyranny has always been a central preoccupation of thinkers and statesmen. Even Thomas Hobbes's ingenious conception of absolute sovereignty, in his view best exemplified by monarchical government, tendered the argument that supreme kingly power could not possibly degenerate into tyranny because of the king's own rationality and because his rule was ultimately founded on the consent of the governed. Out of his own rational self-interest, he would not act tyrannically to the detriment of his subjects, for if he did so over an extended period his throne and life would soon be forfeited. Since Plato, and including Plato in his last monumental work, the *Laws*, thinkers have been much more sceptical than Hobbes about absolutism of any kind, devoting many of their speculations to the question. Between their proposals and the work of politicians and statesmen over the centuries, many remedies for tyranny have been devised and actually embodied in governmental arrangements. Among them have been the rule of law, the mixed constitution, the written constitution, the separation of powers with checks and balances, federalism and the division of powers, an independent judiciary, periodic free elections, legislative responsibility, a party system, legal guarantees of individual rights, and, most recently, democracy.

To recapitulate briefly the problem of tyranny in relation to democracy: only fairly recently has democracy been widely acclaimed to be a bulwark against tyranny. Until the last two centuries, most thinkers and commentators fearful of tyranny were among the most outspoken critics of democracy. Most political theorists and actors, whether by word or deed, displayed an upper-class disdain for the 'vulgar herd' and feared that a democracy dominated by such people would soon degenerate into tyranny. From the nineteenth century onwards this antipathy to democracy eroded until its reversal today. Democracy is praised for being a bastion against tyranny.

Now democracy has become the convenient political slogan of those on all sides of an issue or of opposite parties in a political dispute. With an almost entirely procedural emphasis on the preservation of individual rights and liberties, together with a lack of interest in substantive questions about the distribution of social power, the meaning of democracy has even been altered to include institutional protections against majority rule. Democracy, in the opinion of some, is equated with capitalism and a market society. Democracy in this form has been transformed into a crucial component of the capitalist mentality, that ideological *sine qua non* of advanced capitalism. Democracy has been widely confused with constitutionalism (including the rule of law). On its long semantic journey, this conflation of democracy with constitutionalism has been among the most important shifts. Quite correctly, constitutionalism has long been thought to be a safeguard against tyranny. But to contend that democracy should embody the principles of constitutionalism, thus keeping tyranny at bay, should by no means suggest that the two are synonymous, for democracy should be much more than constitutionalism.

2

At the beginning of the twenty-first century old tyranny still flourishes throughout the world, with no sign of retreat. As soon as one tyranny seems at last to have ended, it is either reinstated, sometimes continuing in a different guise, or another springs up elsewhere. Along with old tyranny and often absorbed by it, advanced capitalism's new tyranny rooted in half a millennium of gradual historical development, first in England and then elsewhere, has gained appreciable momentum since the Second World War. Now that the Soviet empire has collapsed, with socialism in decline, with the Cold War's end, the termination of the nuclear threat, and with the yet unrivalled economic, political and military global domination by the United States, humanity is being subjected to the new tyranny of triumphal capitalism.

The tremendous power of advanced capitalism's new and unprecedented tyranny rests squarely on its total economic organization of society. The production of goods and services in farm, factory and office through an ever changing and increasingly sophisticated technology entails the appropriation of the workers' labour power by capital. This capitalist appropriation is made in exchange for wages in the output of a vast range of commodities to be sold in the market at prices covering productive costs and profits for the owners of the enterprise. Capitalist owners of the means of production always aim at making their commodities competitive in the market – wherever possible eliminating competitors and gaining a monopoly – and at the same time maximizing their profits and reducing their losses. Such a goal is ideally achieved by raising efficiency and increasing labour discipline, constantly revolutionizing productive techniques, cutting the size of the labour force and labour costs. Labour itself becomes a commodity to be bought and sold in the market. Life outside the enterprise is constantly more subject to the imperatives of capitalism that make substantial inroads in every sphere of human life and activity: political, social and cultural. Capitalist values and beliefs permeate all segments of society. Everything and everybody are commodified for sale and purchase. A market price is set on all. Every aspect of life is engulfed by the universalist logic of capitalism and the relentless drive for ever greater profits for fewer and fewer. Nothing is immune to the permeation of capitalism. The whole system of domination thus described is ideologically strengthened and increased by the cultivation of the capitalist mentality, in no small part due to capitalist control of the mass media and cultural life of all kinds.

Advanced capitalism's new tyranny is in many respects far more subtle, more insidious, more hidden from general view, less easily identifiable than old tyranny, determining and shaping the lives of everyone, including those still under the yoke of old tyranny. The new tyranny is not simply the iron fist in the velvet glove. What could be more seductive and disarming than the insinuation of the new tyranny into every facet of human activity and thought under the beguiling cover of democracy, legal and juridicial equality, individual freedom, equality of opportunity, classlessness and progress? People seldom realize that democracy has masked capitalist tyranny in the workplace. Many of us spend most of our working hours under the tyrannical aegis of capitalism in office and factory. When we return home from our labours we are subject to movies, TV and radio – entertainment shaped by the very same capitalism ruling us during the day in the workplace. Democracy seems to be something external to and far removed from our real lives, having little to do with our daily bread and butter. The new tyranny of advanced capitalism is even more total than totalitarianism's old tyranny without, obviously, its horrifying violence and terror, death marches and concentration camps. The new tyranny is totalitarianism with a human face, even though the face is a cleverly contrived mask only designed to appear human and beneficent.

The dynamic of totalizing capitalist tyranny and its subversive hold over the minds and bodies of so many is the principle of avarice, an ingeniously concealed avarice without limits. Capitalism has turned the world of human relations topsy-turvy. Capitalism, as we have seen, legitimizes and institutionalizes greed for money and possessions so roundly denounced by pagan and Christian moralists of past ages. Once firmly established and grounded, and with the elimination of any troublesome opposition, capitalism means that avarice and its concomitant of social disunity are no longer frightening prospects. Capitalism opens up a vista of pleasant and beguiling dreams. What was once feared to be the indisputable symptom of social decay and illness is now exalted for being the sure sign of social health and energy. The fascinating allure of capitalism and the motive power of its tyranny over our lives are its idealization of the lust for profit and possessions as the be-all and end-all of human existence. An entirely new ethos for humankind has been fashioned by capitalism, an ethos of individual pleasure, to be attained by the accumulation of money and possessions. Individual pleasure conceived in these terms becomes the most cherished and sought-after goal of human life. Without such an inversion of values, the new tyranny of capitalism would be unable to maintain its totalitarian grip on our lives. Any serious doubts, anxieties and critical questioning on a widespread scale, if allowed to infiltrate and seize hold of the capitalist mentality, would emasculate the new tyranny, reducing its vitality to helpless impotence. This is why capitalism and its agents take such infinite pains in nourishing the capitalist mentality and its ideology.

One of the chief differences between old tyranny and new tyranny is that the latter increasingly defies personalization. Under old tyranny the abusers of power and authority are easily identifiable. They can be pointed out and named, and once removed from power, their tyranny comes to an end, at least for the time being. But who are the culprits today under advanced capitalism's new tyranny? Are they the large shareholders of the gigantic corporations, stock exchange members, bankers, brokers, corporate chief executive officers and board members, small shareholders and investors, politicians, publishers? Who are those responsible for the new tyranny? Because of the fragmentation and dispersal of corporate ownership and control, naming the true architects of the new tyranny, let alone removing them, would seem to be a virtual impossibility. In any case, anyone involved in capitalist enterprise, whatever their personal disposition, must obey the impersonal imperatives of capitalism just to stay in business – the imperatives of competition and profit maximization. And what of those who may be disillusioned with capitalism and are critical of it, but who at the same time must accept it since they depend upon pensions and retirement investments arranged by their employers? The remarkable feature of the new tyranny is that we are all caught up in and ensnared by the system. The new tyranny of advanced capitalism in a way resembles the many-headed Hydra of ancient Greek mythology, used by Plato in his denunciation of democracy. As soon as one head is severed, another immediately grows in its place.

Advanced capitalism may very well be an abstraction of the activities and mentalities of a vast multitude of individuals and groups. To label capitalism nameless and faceless, an abstraction in this sense, in no way makes it less real or less tyrannical than old tyranny. Capitalism is an abstraction of the activities and mentalities of the innumerable individuals under its sway. They include an exceedingly small minority of the very wealthy and relatively affluent who control and profit enormously from the system, and whose own luxurious comfort and personal security depend upon it. The overwhelming majority, however, in comparison to their capitalist masters must struggle daily for their well-being and even survival. Without their mental and physical labour the system would collapse. Yet they have no option but to persevere and struggle on. In a sense they are collaborators with the new tyranny because they cannot do otherwise. They are caught up in the system, so subject to its total regimen that they are compelled to collaborate, victims, if unwilling ones, because at worst starvation must be avoided, and at best a modicum of well-being attained. All of us, whether or not we are aware of it, whether or not we like it, are at once the victims and in varying degrees the pillars of capitalism's new tyranny. All of us living and working under capitalism, from those large beneficiaries like the very rich and their well-to-do acolytes to the majority eking out a hand-to-mouth existence, are cogs in the machine of capitalism's new tyranny. All of us have been caught up in the ever tightening web of self-tyranny, the tyranny of ourselves over ourselves. We are all ensnared in the inescapable web of capitalism, subject to its totalizing tyranny while at the same time in different degrees we ourselves help to spin that web. In one way or another capitalism consumes all its children, forcing them to devour themselves. We seem to be doomed to the order of the graveyard, to paraphrase Montesquieu's apt description of despotism, because capitalism's new and expanding tyranny, apart from the immense suffering and numerous hardships it incurs, demeans, dehumanizes and devalues the human being. Capitalism's new tyranny contaminates all that it touches. Capitalism, so universalizing in its moulding of our lives, whether we are conscious or not of its all-enveloping thraldom, offers little hope of escape, except more of the same in an ever mounting crescendo.

How has this frightening new tyranny become so deeply rooted? Frightening, primarily to those fortunate enough to be able to rise above the fray and survey the social scene from some vista of relative detachment; not so frightening to the countless others, so caught up in and placidly accepting of the dehumanizing routine, the drudgery and the insecurity of their lives, confronting their lot with a misplaced fortitude, consoling themselves, despite all evidence to the contrary, that they are travelling the inevitable road of liberty, opportunity, merit, classlessness and progress. They have no other option in a regime that so confidently boasts of ever expanding economic growth and freedom of choice. Growth to what end and to whose advantage?

Freedom of choice in regard to what may be the least essential, a perpetual merry-go-round of enticing and often useless consumer goods, not to the crucial shaping and direction of our lives. The majority at the bottom of the social pyramid, often ill-nourished, ill-clothed, ill-housed, without adequate medical care, mentally and physically exhausted by the far-reaching capitalist tyranny, must find consolation in the vain prospect of being lucky enough to better themselves, perhaps by winning at the races or in the lottery.

How then have we been trapped in the cul-de-sac of advanced capitalism and held captive by its new tyranny? Is it because capitalism appeals to what used to be called the 'baser impulses' of humankind, unleashing, organizing and legitimizing them? Now these so-called baser impulses are exalted, eulogized and promoted by every imaginable means at the disposal of those who operate the levers of power. The emphasis is on the self, upon enhancing the pleasures of the individual in the perpetual and self-destructive quest for money and possessions. So the perilous dehumanizing process continues producing an ever more inequitable society and an ever more compliant and subservient government masquerading as democracy.

Part II

THE AMERICAN NATION

5

PORTENTS OF SOCIAL DECAY

Viewed from afar, the United States – 'the greatest democracy in the world' – is a frightening society. For those who are caught up in and habituated to its frenzied pace and brutal atomism, America is accepted as a haven of freedom and security. Yet some doubts are beginning to appear as to whether something isn't basically wrong. Typical is the masterly understatement of George F. Kennan in the *New York Review of Books* of 11 August 1999: 'We are not, really, all that great. We have serious problems within our society these days'. Is it indeed the kind of society that the founding fathers envisioned? Doubts have arisen, especially since the Oklahoma City bombing of a federal office building and the spate of killings of schoolchildren by their classmates in the late 1990s, not to mention racist-motivated gunning down of people on the streets. Detached global onlookers shudder at the violence that is seemingly endemic in American society, at the grossness of much of American behaviour at home and abroad, and at the banal mindlessness of so much of the culture. Is this what is in store for the rest of the world, now that the United States is the sole superpower presiding over the globalization of the international economy, ready to deploy its unsurpassed military might against any state seemingly threatening its imperialist expansionism? As the planet becomes increasingly Americanized, is this the kind of earthly 'paradise' that people everywhere must anticipate in the not too distant future? The gigantic urban sprawl and squalor of Los Angeles, despoiling a once beautiful natural environment, may very well suggest what we can anticipate, in the words of Mike Davis's *Ecology of Fear*: '500 gated sub-divisions, 2,000 street gangs, 4,000 mini-malls, 20,000 sweatshops, and 100,000 homeless residents'. Los Angeles, with its overwhelming car culture, shoot-outs on the motorways, and endless miles of atrocious buildings and consumer outlets, is not America, but what is happening to it may well be a harbinger of the future of the United States and possibly even of humanity. Moreover, the launch of the war against terrorism in response to the disaster of 11 September, and the collapse of Enron, the exposure of WorldCom and Xerox, and the revelations about other corporate shenanigans are far from reassuring. A closer look at American society should indicate why the prospect before us is bleak and fearsome. I wish, therefore, to begin by outlining some of the features of the social structure and public health of the United States. This is followed by a discussion of violence, consumerism, the frenetic pace of American life fuelled by reliance on car travel, cellular phones, the Internet and computers, ending with some thoughts about culture in a narrow sense and about higher education. While many volumes could be written on these subjects, such a synoptic view should give us pause for reflection.

1

Without question the most disturbing aspect of American society is a burgeoning and unprecedented inequality, possibly even more disturbing than the escalating violence. The two are causally linked because the coexistence of widespread poverty and deprivation with the colossal riches of a few and their extravagant conspicuous consumption constitute an explosive social mixture. How such a nation, by far the world's richest, combining so much poverty and such a concentration of wealth, can be called democratic is simply incomprehensible. The gap between the many poor and the very small minority of the extremely rich is widening at an alarming rate. The United States remains, and is increasingly, a class society based on wealth and its privileges. An exact calculation of the class divisions of American society, based on income and other relevant factors, is obviously extremely difficult. But, at a rough estimate, we can say that approximately 25 per cent are poor, of whom some are close to destitution. At the other extreme 20 per cent are wealthy, of whom 10 per cent are very wealthy. In between is what Americans like to call the 'middle class', which includes large numbers of workers, some of whom earn very modest wages.

We begin our imprecise sketch with the 25 per cent or less at the bottom of the social hierarchy. Many of them, especially the truly impoverished, have little or no job security, live below a 'comfortable adequacy', and lack any kind of medical cover, often afflicted with diseases otherwise found only in Third World countries. Functional illiteracy and innumeracy, while growing throughout American society, seem largely to be concentrated in this group. Now that the welfare state is being dismantled and with middle- and upper-class demands for tax cuts, balanced budgets, fiscal responsibility and further privatization, the war of the rich against the poor has finally been won, to refer to a recent comment by John Kenneth Galbraith.

About 50 per cent of the poor live below the 'poverty level', 12.7 per cent of the total population according to the 1998 census. These poor are considerably poorer than in most other industrialized nations. Of those at or below the poverty level, a third suffer from hunger and malnutrition. Paradoxically, in the world's wealthiest country, soup kitchens, food pantries and food banks are increasing at a perilous rate. To save many from hunger, they are proliferating on Indian reservations, in rural areas, suburbs and large cities. Even in the nation's wealthiest state, Connecticut, thousands of poor and working people have to resort to soup kitchens, and their numbers are increasing. In 2001 the largest American private hunger relief agency and its affiliates fed twenty-three million people. The problem is compounded by the fact that only about 40 per cent of the unemployed are eligible to draw unemployment benefits. More than one-half of the impoverished are equally divided between blacks and Hispanics. Less than 10 per cent are non-Hispanic whites, and the rest are Asians or Pacific Islanders. Members of the lower class, if fortunate enough to be employed, are in low-wage and unskilled jobs, working long hours. In general, American workers labour longer hours than their European counterparts.

Unemployment figures in the United States, the lowest of any advanced industrial nation, though increasing, tend to be rather deceptive. While about twelve million, or 5 per cent of the total population, are unemployed, several other categories should perhaps be added to this number. Six million people are in 'contingent' or temporary jobs. Fifteen million who need full-time work hold reduced or part-time jobs without benefits. In addition, three million or more are unemployed but are not included in the statistics because they have not qualified for benefits or because they have given up looking for work. Then there are over two million in the swelling prison population, although many of these are forced to labour. The grand total of those who are either unemployed, engaged in part-time jobs, in the armed forces or in prison amounts to 10–15 per cent of the total population. This figure does not include the nearly one million child labourers, some as young as seven years old, working as underpaid farmhands, dishwashers, in laundries or as domestics. Some of them work as much as ten hours a day, clearly in violation of the Child Labor Laws.

Moving up the social scale, the next 20–30 per cent (along with the employed among the lower 25 per cent of the population) comprise the skilled and high-waged labour force that supplies the labour power so necessary to keep the capitalist system going. Although this stratum may live in 'comfortable adequacy', job security seems to be a relic of the past. Average blue-collar and white-collar workers are no longer assured of retaining their jobs until retirement. Those who are laid off or 'downsized' are urged to be 'flexible' and to 'retool', often at their own expense, or to leave their community and seek work where jobs are more plentiful. Labour union membership, the traditional guarantor of workers' rights and interests and a major protagonist in the struggle for democracy since nineteenth-century industrialization, has fallen in the United States from 40 per cent after the Second World War, to 12–15 per cent today, far less than in most other advanced industrial countries. 'Union bashing' is a favourite tactic of the upper classes, political parties and government. We are told from all sides that unions threaten freedom and hinder social progress. Belonging to a union and active involvement in its activities practically carries the well-worn stigma of being 'un-American'. No one, of course, dares mention that we are in fact dominated by the tyranny of capitalist enterprise, or that it is much more dangerous for our liberties than organized labour. Socialism (the very term chills the marrow of better-off Americans), long a defender of workers against tyrannical capitalism, has long been in retreat, and there is no sign of the emergence of a strong well-organized Labor Party. The Republican and Democratic parties (except perhaps for the small liberal wing of the Democrats) have become virtually identical, converging to the right of the political centre's spectrum. Both are ardent supporters of capitalism and free enterprise, and manage to ignore the plight of American workers.

White-collar workers are just as insecure in their jobs as blue-collar workers. 'Downsizing' in the hunt for ever greater corporate profits by streamlining and rationalizing business operations is standard practice in the offices as well as the factories of small and large concerns. Women have increasingly entered the workforce, often compelled to do so as single parents or to help their partners (laid off or working) to support the family. The bulk of the labour force is non-union, much of it part time: because of low wages, workers may have to hold down two or more jobs to make ends meet. Many adults, men and women, work in sweatshop conditions, and child labour blots the social landscape. The homeless stand on city street corners begging in all weather, a warning to employed workers of their own fate if they do not toe the line. The beggars without beds in shelters not infrequently freeze to death when sleeping rough during freezing weather.

Here, then, are the 'ordinary Americans', who in the past would have been identified with the 'working class', but since the United States, supposedly, is a 'classless society' the expression is taboo. An exception, however, is made because most Americans, even many workers, like to think of themselves as 'middle class'. The middle class, however, in any traditional use of the term, designates the next higher stratum of about 25 per cent, consisting of business managers, corporate bureaucrats, civil servants, highly skilled technicians and professionals like lawyers, architects, engineers, doctors, dentists, teachers, nurses and scientists. Most are college and university graduates, whose wages by virtue of a degree alone are about 70 per cent higher than those of the average high school graduate. Except for the wealthy, all incomes have declined annually in real terms since the early 1990s, including those of this middle class. Middle-class people have generally forsaken living in the central urban cores (except in New York City), moving to the suburbs where they run at least two cars, sometimes more. Middle-class wives often work, depositing young children in daycare centres and nurseries, and relying on house cleaning by domestics. The middle class habitually demand lower taxes (even though the rate at the time of writing is well below any of the advanced nations), minimal government, balanced budgets and more privatization. Their children are provided with costly higher education in order to launch them properly into the higher income adult market-place.

At the pinnacle of the social structure are the wealthy, another 20 per cent of the whole, of whom the top 10 per cent are the truly wealthy. Included in this stratum are bankers, stockbrokers, corporate executives, publishers, affluent lawyers and other top professionals. They live luxuriously in palatial multiple residences, travel extensively, some in their private jets, and relish conspicuous consumption of the most costly kind. They constitute a ruling class in the customary sense with a decisive political influence. The average income of the top 15 per cent soared by over 80 per cent, after taxes, between the 1980s, and the early 2000s, while income of the bottom 20 per cent declined by 10 per cent. Of those over the age of sixteen, the top 800,000 have more money and other assets than the rest of the population combined. In 1980, in no state of the United States was the average income of the wealthiest 20 per cent of families more than ten times that of the poorest quintile. The disparity is now greater than 1:13 if the poorest families with children are considered. While three out of five households have lost real income since 1985, the top 20 per cent increased their real income by 28 per cent and the richest 1 per cent almost doubled their real income. In 1998, the average company executive out-earned his workers by 200:1, compared to 40:1 in 1977. The median compensation of the top executives of the 350 biggest corporations is about sixty times greater than the median family income of nearly $40,000 a year. In 1997, 68 per cent of the total federal tax cut went to the top 1 per cent of earners. Millionaires are now, as it were, 'a dime a dozen': the figure must be in the neighbourhood of three million. Billionaires are a much rarer species, but still relatively plentiful. In our world there are 465 billionaires. Of the top ten, seven are Americans; and among the top one hundred, forty-one are American. Microsoft founder and co-chairman Bill Gates is the richest person in the world, worth $90 billion. The world's top two hundred billionaires' wealth more than doubles the $463 billion of the two hundred leading billionaires of 1990.

The United States, then, is quite clearly a hierarchical class society. Class is determined not by family, education or ability, but by wealth and the facility to acquire wealth. Approximately one quarter of the people are poor and by all accounts growing poorer, living in insecurity and crime, ill-housed and ill-clothed, and without proper medical attention. Their chances of rising in the hierarchy are virtually nil. Social and income upward mobility is no higher in the United States than in Europe and indeed may be worse. American society is more inegalitarian than that of most other advanced industrial countries. More are living in poverty than in Europe, Canada and Japan. The poor, in fact, are disfranchised, for why should they bother to vote since their condition is only worsening? At the apex of the social pyramid are the rich, growing ever richer, who control the levers of political power and public opinion. Is this a classless society? Can this possibly be the world's 'greatest democracy', a society polarized between the very poor and the very rich, with inegalitarianism constantly increasing? We are forever being reminded by the media controlled by the rich and their henchmen, the politicians, that this is the road to freedom and progress, the nursery of personal responsibility, initiative and industry, of the self-made and vigorous capitalist men and women of the future. Obviously no one tells us that if all who live in such misery, or even a relatively small percentage of them, were to become capitalists, no one would be left to perform the menial, repetitive, arduous and oppressive labour upon which capitalism so depends. All of this, however, as we shall see, is only part of the dismal American scene under advanced capitalism's new tyranny. Nevertheless Will Hutton reports that Richard Grasco, president of the New York Stock Exchange, proclaimed in 1997 that 'Americans should not deny the fact that of all the nations in the history of the world theirs is the most just, the most tolerant … and the best model for the future'.

As America becomes wealthier and increasingly imperialist, a class society polarized between a handful of the very rich and many very poor, the physical and mental health of citizens has declined. Again, the contrast is often between the very many poor and the wealthy minority. Over forty million people, or about 15 per cent of the population, on any day of the year have no adequate medical coverage, and as many as seven million have none on a permanent basis. On the other hand, the well-to-do and affluent are amply covered by expensive health insurance for themselves and their families, either privately purchased or obtained through their employment. Many under the age of eighteen living in families above the poverty level are uninsured, a figure that appears to be mounting because employers have reduced or eliminated health insurance coverage for employees' dependants. It is scandalous that the world's 'greatest democracy', the richest and most powerful on earth, should not have an adequate non-profit healthcare system like most advanced industrial nations: Canada, Britain, Scandinavia and the rest of western Europe. In the United States, however, private health insurance companies are engaged for profit in a lucrative capitalist enterprise to the detriment of the public welfare. Over four million American children, many on welfare, suffer from malnutrition, and even brain damage often resulting from inadequate prenatal and infant nourishment. In general, healthcare for the poor and needy has been reduced because so many counties forced to pare their budgets have been closing health-care centres. In some states, over 20 per cent of the population has no health insurance in comparison to 10 per cent in some of the more affluent and provident states. Is this a people's democracy?

The lower classes are hit much more heavily than the well-to-do by a variety of health problems. Possibly a million or more die annually from alcohol abuse, tobacco-related diseases, diabetes and pollution. This is apart from the affliction of AIDS, a leading cause of death among black adults between the ages of twenty-five and forty-four, often resulting from drug injections. Ten million or more have serious drinking problems, not confined to the poor. Again, the well-to-do share with the poor in taking hard drugs on a regular basis. Likewise with the use of marijuana, some being heavy users: the figure is over 12 per cent. Obesity and weight problems in every class, but primarily among those in the lower strata, are on an upswing, affecting over one in five adult women and one in four adult men, possibly due to an unbalanced diet and the constant nibbling of snacks, pizzas, sweets, fried foods, etc. About 300,000 deaths per year are reported from obesity or related causes. More than ten million, largely among the poor, suffer from symptomatic asthma. The figure is shooting up rapidly because of the polluted air, one of the penalties of living in a car culture with its ever growing network of highways and the decline of efficient systems of public transport. Manufacturing plants are also prime culprits. Life expectancy in the United States is lower than it is in France, Germany, Italy and Britain.

Those living comfortably, and the affluent and wealthy, are obviously not immune from many of these health hazards. Physical fitness has become their watchword, encouraged by profit-making health clubs and exercise centres. In large cities and small, in parks and on pavements and in the streets, numerous joggers labour on with their head-sets and cellular phones, then, after finishing their run, go home by car, shower and go to work.

But the upper classes are certainly not free from their own health concerns. The constant stress and anxiety of contemporary life under the tyranny of capitalism is taking its toll, in the first instance more on the minds than on the bodies of comfortably-off Americans. 'Go to a shrink' is the usual advice from friends and family. Fifty years ago, hardly anyone – and then it was a closely guarded secret – ever contemplated consulting a psychiatrist. Far different today, for psychiatry and counselling are booming, profitable businesses. About one-third of the population have sought some sort of psychological counselling during their lifetime. Today, more than one in ten seek help from psychiatric, psychotherapeutic or medical services for mental or emotional problems at a cost of over $4 billion annually. More than one in six, mostly women, use emotion-controlling drugs. Mental illness, of course, is not confined to the upper classes alone. At least a quarter of a million (largely, but not only, the poor) are institutionalized. At the same time a similar number are released, due to local budget cutbacks, to exist mainly in flophouses or on the streets.

One might even be tempted to claim that the United States seems to be in danger of becoming one vast 'loony-bin' of self-centred, brainwashed, grossly overweight men, women and children, who, because of the incessant street noise, the screeching music in every café, restaurant and bar, and the thunderous sound of movies and TV, are losing their hearing. Americans, comprising 'the indispensable nation', in the words of Madeleine Albright, the former Secretary of State, are threatened on every side by the decay of their culture. Can this be the stuff of a vibrant, informed democracy?

2

What strikes most outside observers about the United States is possibly not so much that it is a highly inegalitarian class society, but that it has a constantly accelerating culture of violence. America can hardly offer itself to the world as the beacon of freedom and democracy it claims to be, to be avidly followed by the planet's billions, as long as this tidal wave of violence is sweeping the streets, the schools, the homes and the prisons, a growing violence that seems to have no end. Violence is everywhere in the United States. The constant backdrop to the actual physical violence occurring every minute of the day is the violence continuously depicted on TV, the violence of the movies with their horror and supernatural films, the latest stories of violence featured in the tabloids. People outside work are mesmerized by the TV coverage of the O. J. Simpson trial and the McVeigh trial in connection with the Oklahoma bombing. The killings of students and teachers in well-to-do public schools and the gunning-down of innocent victims on urban pavements has incited public consternation over the lax gun laws and the prodigious lobbying of the National Rifle Association and produced vast amounts of news articles and editorial comment engaging in self-examination. Why has America been afflicted with such a plague of violence and killing, and even more since about 1990? Why do so many American suburbanites live in over three million gated compounds? Why are schoolchildren in the schools of large urban centres screened for carrying firearms in the classrooms? Why are some women university undergraduates, for example, at Mt Holyoke College, an elite institution, carrying hand-guns?

That violence has become so much a part of life of Americans does not mean that they are naturally violent. A people is never innately violent. They become violent because of a variety of circumstances. Social conditions under which they live are often productive of vio-lence. A social environment of vast disparities of wealth and income, of mounting poverty, poor housing and declining health, of increasing stress and strain in the workplace, is an incubator of vio-lence. A major factor in the United States seems to be the unrelenting ruthlessness of the new tyranny of advanced capitalism. It is perhaps a sign of the times that the spokesmen of capitalism resort to the lan-guage of violence, of warfare, the most extreme manifestation of violence, in describing business operations, its tactics and strategy. John R. MacArthur, the publisher of *Harper's Magazine*, gives us examples of this business rhetoric of violence: 'targeting markets', 'making killings', 'slashing costs', 'destroying the competition', sur-viving 'foreign assaults on US markets'.

In the *Financial Times* of London, an article by Peter Martin, 'Lessons in Humility' (22 June 1999), begins with a quote from General Colin Powell: 'Remember – soldiers are warriors'. Martin proceeds to argue that business people should (like warriors) have a sense of mission. A successful company must cultivate the 'self-image' that it consists of the 'good guys', concluding: 'Being a warrior is all very well but as General Powell would be the first to accept, you need to be fighting on someone's behalf, not just for yourself'. The same newspaper, during the summer of 1999, published each week the 'Financial Times Library of Business Classics'. Although Machiavelli's *The Prince* has long been a favourite of businessmen, the *Financial*

Times launched its Business Classics on 27 July 1999 with Sun Tzu's *The Art of War*. Its billing was: 'Written 2,500 years ago, this warrior handbook explores the psychology of conflict and is an allegory for modern management'. A brief introduction states:

> Written for Chinese generals, his maxims on strategy and lea-dership – with a good pinch of ruthlessness – offer sharp lessons for modern managers ... *The Art of War* has many exponents in business. Michael Ovitz, the Hollywood agent, gives all his senior executives copies of the book.

Several excerpts chosen at random convey something of the flavour of the book:

> All warfare is based on deception. ... Humble words and increased preparations are signs that the enemy is about to advance. ... Therefore, soldiers must be treated in the first instance, with humanity, but kept under control by means of iron discipline. ... He who exercises no forethought but makes light of his opponents is sure to be captured by them.

It seems that capitalism is war employing money instead of bullets.

The statistics on American violence are simply overwhelming, although the violent crime rate, at least so we are informed, has been appreciably declining over the last two to three years. Thanks to the prodigious efforts of the National Rifle Association since the early 1970s and its buying of many congressmen, no adequate compre-hensive laws regulating firearms sales exist in the United Sates, unlike most advanced societies. Recently, several states including California have, however, attempted to control the sale of firearms. At least half of American households own firearms, with some 200 million handguns alone, not to mention more dangerous automatic weapons.

More than 100,000 children take guns to school. In 1990–92, the murder rate was 1 per 100,000, the figure having tripled since 1950. The United States leads the industrialized world by a long way in this regard. The figure may have been declining in recent years, but 20,000 murders were committed in 1995: 68 per cent by firearms, of which 82 per cent were handguns. Every two years perhaps as many as 50,000 Americans are killed by guns. In 1994, 1,464 homicides were committed by American children. Thirteen million are victims of other crimes: assault, rape, robbery, burglary, larceny, arson. In 1997, 85,000 people were wounded by firearms, of whom 38,000 died, including 2,600 children. Suicide rates are also exceptionally high in comparison with the rest of the world. Since 1950, suicide rates have quadrupled. In 1997, there were 27,000 suicides. In the industrialized world in 1994, six hundred young children were reported to have committed suicide, over half being in the United States. In sum, the United States had by far the highest rates of homicides, firearms-related deaths and suicides compared with the rest of the world's twenty-six richest nations.

Cars and highways certainly have a share in deaths and serious injuries. Nearly 50,000 are killed, and almost two million suffer non-fatal injuries each year in automobile accidents. Of those injured, over 150,000 suffer permanent impairments. A new phenomenon has proliferated on the nation's roads, labelled 'aggressive driving' or in British parlance 'road rage'. Between 1990 and 1996, there were over 10,000 reported incidents of aggressive driving, over 200 killed and over 12,000 injured. Roads have become the 'Wild West', with people pressed for time, rushing from home to work or from work to home. Such aggression may be exhibited against drivers who cut off another car when changing lanes, who go too slowly in the outside lane, and who tail-gate. In California, shots have been exchanged between speeding cars on the freeways. Apart from deaths and injuries, well over 1.25 million cars are stolen annually, thefts amounting to £7 billion each year. All told, then, more than 100,000 lose their lives annually from homicide, suicide and automobile accidents, more deaths than the United States armed forces incurred in the Second World War, Korea and Vietnam, and far outstripping deaths from such causes in the other industrialized countries.

Murders, suicides and deaths on the highway are not the only testimony to the American culture of violence. The statistics on violence against women, children and the elderly are simply appalling. Between two and four million women a year are battered. Domestic violence is the single largest cause of injury and the second cause of death for women. At least two women are raped every minute of the day. Forty million Americans, one of every four women and one of every ten men, are estimated to have been sexually abused as children, most commonly between the ages of nine and twelve, usually by relatives or family acquaintances. About three million children annually are reportedly subject to serious neglect or abuse, including physical torture and deliberate starvation. More than 30,000 children suffer permanent physical disability through abuse and neglect. Five thousand children are killed annually by parents or grandparents. Over one million children kept in orphanages, reformatories and adult prisons are abused. Children are actually jailed, committed without due process, for minor transgressions. Approximately two million elderly people living within their families are seriously abused, involving forcible confinement, underfeeding and beatings. A large but undetermined number of the over one million elderly people confined to nursing homes – established to make the greatest profits – often live in conditions of extreme neglect, filth and abuse.

In order to contain and reduce this avalanche of violence, the United States seems to have only one answer: incarceration, and for the most serious offences, the death penalty. The creation of a social environment free from poverty and disease, strengthening the educational system, improved housing, a universal health programme, and strict gun laws might not eliminate the endemic violence in American society, but if actually implemented should go a long way towards correcting the situation. This, of course, would require an enormous outlay of public funds, and in an ethos of reducing taxes, balanced budgets, minimizing governmental functions and more privatization, the response is in the negative. More prisons and more death sentences are the answer. Vengeance upon those who have transgressed seems to be a primary motive for the expanding number of prisons and prison inmates. We know from experience and many studies that this approach, including stricter penalties, simply does not deter crime. The over two million in prisons – proportionately more than any other industrialized country – helps solve the employment problem. Greed is also an important factor, for prisons have to be built, and the more prisons the greater profits for private builders. In 1997, three new prisons were built every week in the United States. Indeed, the construction of new prisons in California is a booming business. Many prisons have been privatized and are operated on the profit motive. Prisoners are a source of cheap labour and are often put to work making goods for the market. In Florida, the 64,000 inmates in 1997 were required to work without remu-neration in chain gangs, making products like boots and licence plates, which are frequently exported to foreign countries. Airlines use prisoners without payment to make seat reservations. With only 5 per cent of the world's population, in 2000 the United States had 25 per cent of the global prison population, over two million inmates, tri-pling since the 1980s, and doubling in the 1990s. Some 60 per cent were from racial minorities and at least 10 per cent of the total were women. Many prisoners are drug offenders, nearly a quarter of the total, of whom a high proportion are black. In California, four out of every ten blacks in their twenties are either jailed or on probation.

Throughout the United States one out of seven were, because of their criminal convictions, permanently or temporarily disfranchised. The state of California, in 1980, spent six times more on its universities than on its prisons. Today more is spent on jails than on universities. Prison wardens commonly earn more than schoolteachers. A good share of the millions spent in the United States on public law enforcement goes to prisons and prison maintenance.

Blistering reports on prison conditions and death row incarceration have started to appear, although they have received scant attention in the American media. Amnesty International, in 1998, and more recently the United Nations Commission on Human Rights, have been devastating in their criticism of American jails, concentrating on the very large number of people held on death row awaiting execution. The number is now over 3,000. For their crimes, minors and mentally retarded individuals are not infrequently subjected to the death penalty, and must wait their turn on death row. In 1997 sixty-five juveniles were in the queues awaiting execution. Women prisoners are often sexually abused, and racial discrimination is rampant. Restraint chairs, leg irons and electric shock weapons (stun guns) are widely used to control prisoners. The reports concentrated mainly on the relatively vast numbers being held for execution, some for many years. A Canadian, for instance, who had waited on death row for two decades, was recently executed in Texas, which has the highest number of executions of any state. Thirty-eight of the fifty states have the death penalty, which has been abolished in all other advanced industrial countries. The only other countries in the world known since 1990 to execute juveniles are Iran, Nigeria, Pakistan, Saudia Arabia and Yemen. Since it is well known that capital punishment does not deter crime, the obvious conclusion is that the prisons, inhumane prison conditions and capital punishment reflect the growing violence of American culture, on the principle of an eye for an eye. Can the United States in clear conscience possibly stand up and condemn the violations of human rights in other countries?

3

The United States is an inegalitarian class society generating a horrifying environment of crime and violence. Much of this seems to have resulted from advanced capitalism's ever expanding tyranny over our thoughts and activities. Capitalism appeals to and unleashes what used to be called the 'baser impulses' of humankind. Today, these baser impulses have been legitimized, are exalted, even eulogized, and promoted by every conceivable means at the disposal of the agents of capitalism's unregenerate tyranny. The emphasis, often ingeniously designed to avoid offending the squeamish, is invariably on the self, on enhancing the pleasure of the individual in the endless chase after money and possessions. No wonder a recent book by Marc Lewis, *Sin to Win* should be doing so well in America. As reported in the *Financial Times* of 18 February 2002, Lewis maintains that 'self-interest is eternal – everybody always wants more'. He is of the opinion that 'vice is essential to success and no one should feel guilty about it. Coveting stops you being complacent.' Shades of Mandeville!

The disease of consumerism has swept through capitalist America, impelled by advertising, the din of the mass media, the ease of borrowing. We are forever being urged to spend and spend, to buy and buy, to invest and invest. Americans, manipulated by the artful agents of capitalism, have been launched on an endless and mindless shopping and buying spree. The value of thrift, so cherished in the past, has been discarded. Americans, whether they can afford to or not, seem always to want more in a vain attempt to satisfy their endless desires. Personal satisfaction and contentment have long been forsaken, as fortunate Americans spend their earnings, often on useless commodities. Capitalism, people are constantly warned, can only survive and thrive on the basis of perpetual spending and consumption. In their race to acquire more and more goods, many Americans seem to be ever unsatisfied. If America is a culture of class, a culture of violence, it is also a culture of consumerism. Everything and everybody have a monetary price, seldom related to their intrinsic worth. The value of everything depends on how much we desire it and are willing to pay for it. Everything and everybody are commodified, to be bought and sold in the market. To facilitate this shopping spree, shops are often open twenty-four hours a day, seven days a week, and Americans are serviced by nearly 30,000 shopping malls. Those who have computers can surf the Internet for the latest bargains in goods and services. Some, who perhaps can least afford it, are the psychological victims of shopping addiction, 'shopping crazy' in a literal sense.

The penalty for the rampant consumerism is the rise of personal bankruptcy and indebtedness. Since 1970–80 bankruptcies have quintupled (in the past due to the relaxation of the law), approaching 1.4 million in 1997. The ratio of personal debt to income (after tax) grew from 59 per cent in 1984 to 83 per cent in 1998. American households apply an average of 17 per cent of disposable income to servicing their debts, just below the record high of 17.6 per cent in 1989. An average of $1,000 a year is spent on credit card interest and fees. The total household debt in 1998 has surged ahead to an astronomical $5.5 trillion. To satisfy further the insatiable demand of consumers, the total worth of imports far exceeds the exports, spiralling now to well over $20 billion a month, a forbidding problem that Americans will have to confront in the future. While congressmen are seriously considering a law requiring the display of the ten commandments in every school classroom in an effort to combat juvenile crime, and while much of the world's population struggles for the bare necessities of life, this circus of consumerism continues unabated.

Our very essence as humans is rapidly being reduced to the appetite for buying, as testified by the logo of a retailers' promotional organization: 'I consume, therefore, I am'. The implications of this gross travesty of the famous Cartesian principle are horrifying. We exist not by virtue of our rationality, as Descartes long ago argued, but because we have been reduced to mindless behavioural mechanisms programmed to the full to partake in a perpetual buying and spending spree. Christmas and Easter are now carnivals of consumerism with much touted 'store sales' tempting customers with a vast array of goods at bargain prices. Newspapers, magazines, TV, telephone, junk mail and flyers, and the Internet all turn life into a gargantuan bazaar. Commercials on TV bombard the viewer. In 1996, 15 minutes 21 seconds were allotted to 'non-programme' material in the average hour, up almost a minute from the previous year. Between a quarter and a third of every hour is devoted to commercial and promotional advertising. Although, during prime time, the viewer is confronted on average with twenty-seven commercials per hour, during the daytime this increases to forty commercials per hour, about one-third of every hour allotted to non-programme material. Built-in obsolescence of goods and constant changes in fashion ranging from clothing to motor cars and computers help fire consumer desire for ever more of the latest. Escape or respite from the constant display of advertising is virtually impossible even if we switch off our TVs and radios. Buses, taxis and even police cars are adorned with the most garishly colourful ads imaginable. Schools and even university lavatory doors are not immune to blandishments designed to entice new customers. Faced by the growing cutback of funds, some universities have resorted to finding corporate sponsors for courses, laboratories and

lecture halls, the name of the business sponsor always given promi-
nence. We are living in a time in which the image takes precedence
over reality. Packaging and promotional drives, logos and brand
names aim to fabricate a saleable appearance for commodities. Indeed
voters elect specific candidates not on their merits or political pro-
grammes, but solely on the grounds of whose image projected on TV
during their term of office would be the least boring and off-putting.
Disneyland appearances seem to be confused with actuality. We are
becoming the robots of virtual reality.

4

To the outsider, the proverbial visitor from another planet, the basic
stuff of American society would appear to be class, with its deep and
widening gulf between the very rich and very poor, the proliferating
crime and violence, and the rampaging and insatiable consumerism
stoked by the media. Another feature of American life must be added
to this trinity: the accelerating, frenetic pace of life, producing what
almost amounts to a culture of frenzy. Relaxation and escape from it
all (even during holidays), the chance to snatch even a brief break
from the job, seem to be increasingly futile, particularly now that
work is much faster and onerous than before. Relaxation and escape
are in danger of vanishing. Work via cellular phone and computer has
invaded our time away from office and home. This new 'interconnectedness', as Thomas Friedman calls it, has demolished our
peace and privacy, and any opportunity to get away from it all. The
cellular phone, now indispensable for every kind of business and
socializing, always keeps us in touch wherever we are, whether driving, walking in the city, jogging, sitting on a park bench, dining in a
restaurant, having a drink in a bar or café, shopping, pushing a baby

buggy, standing at a urinal, or even walking through the countryside. There is no escape. Cellular phones are only part of the story of the 'interconnectedness' that has swept America and threatens the end of privacy, peace and relaxation. The increasing use of computers in the office, work site, home and while travelling, heightens tensions everywhere and exacerbates the frenzied rat-race that life has become. The United States has more computers than the rest of the world combined, and 26 per cent of the population regularly surf the Internet. We no longer write friends and colleagues carefully crafted letters composed after due thought and consideration. Instead we bombard them from morning to night with messages via email, which almost verge on a perpetual stream of consciousness. Where will it all end, and how will it affect our individual and collective psyches?

A crucial contributor to the culture of frenzy is the car. To make ends meet and to facilitate our consumer madness, people whip their cars along city streets and country roads at breakneck speed, weaving in and out of traffic, drivers of every sex and age furiously displaying their machismo by honking defiantly at every obstacle (other vehicles and pedestrians) blocking their forward path. An absolute 'car mania' (to purloin the title of a book by Winfried Wolf) seems to have seized the populace in advanced capitalist countries and especially the United States, where it all began. The American love affair with the car and the necessity of automotive transport in most places have succeeded in restructuring our culture in numerous ways. The car obsession fuels and intensifies the other traits of American society, underwriting class, violence and consumerism, increasing the frenetic pace of life, and becoming a pillar of the capitalist productive process.

The shape of American society resulting from endemic car mania over the last century defies the imagination. Car density in the United States far outstrips any of the other advanced capitalist countries. As car density has skyrocketed, travel by rail and other means of public transport has been underfunded and has appreciably declined. A mass exodus of the affluent and comfortably-off from the central urban core to suburbia has brought significant changes to the structure of the American city. Much of the countryside adjacent to towns and cities has been blemished by broad freeways, criss-crossing at spaghetti junctions. Large shopping centres have mushroomed near the freeways to service the needs of suburban residents, with gigantic car parks to accommodate eager purchasers. Students now often drive to secondary and high school and universities, their campuses covered with car parks and parking structures.

Middle-class families, particularly since wives as well as husbands are working, have at least two cars, and often three, if not four, once the children reach their teens. Even working-class families living on the fringes of suburbia often have two cars. The kind of car, if not the number, is still a status symbol, families with Mercedes, BMWs and Volvos constituting a driving elite. Car-washing establishments enable drivers on the move to have their vehicles in immaculate condition. Petrol-guzzling 'recreation vehicles', in addition to regular cars, are required by families with small children and generally for shopping. Since old urban neighbourhoods with small shops have all but vanished, shopping by car at the gargantuan shopping centres is essential. And always nearby are drive-in restaurants and other establishments with car service. Added to the substantial alteration in the physical and man-made environments, and the transformation of social life, car mania is a hazardous affair, creating dangerous air pollution and related health hazards, spawning crime and violence, and 'joy-riding' teenagers, not to mention the many road accidents and deaths. 'War on the streets' or 'road rage' is a relatively recent occurrence, with, in its most extreme form, irate drivers actually shooting and killing each other. A popular news magazine, described in 1987, the southern Californian highways as becoming 'a zone of terror'. The revolution wrought by car mania should not be minimized, nor should the powerful political voice exerted by car manufacturers, producers of automobile accessories, and oil and petrol companies, who together are the foundation of the American capitalist system.

The frantic race of American life brought about by the high priority given to business and money-making among members of the middle and upper classes (let alone the lower classes' necessity of economic survival) and impelled by the interconnectedness made possible by the cellular phone and computer and by car mania, has diminished rather than enhanced the quality of life. Conversations at adjoining tables in restaurants, cafés and bars are seldom worth overhearing. Instead of interesting observations – much less sparkling repartee – on the arts, religion, politics and national and international events, discussions invariably have to do with buying and selling, marketing and packaging, financial transactions and stock market, office and corporate structuring and restructuring. All of this is frequently interrupted by cellular phone calls. The constant transfusion renewing America's life blood via car, phone and computer seems to have but one frenetic purpose: to make money and to spend money. The hectic bazaar of buying and selling produces bazaar mentalities, or such might be the judgment of the visitor from Mars. Classical music radio stations, at least the few surviving ones, now feature 'shows', not 'programs'. Movements are extracted from symphonies, the music interspersed with the banal chatter of announcers and the equal banality of commercials. A fragment of a Brahms symphony ends with advertisements for Lysol and haemorrhoidal suppositories, then on to Ravel, to be followed by disquisitions on the use of Aspirin and the advantage of a particular brand of sanitary towel, before J.S. Bach. The few non-commercial stations can survive only by means of endless and tedious fund-raising drives. Civility on pavements and streets, in the clamour of stores, and in reactions to strangers has noticeably declined in urban areas. The sterile conformity of American life is no better symbolized than by the popular eating and drinking tastes: the 'Big Mac', the pizza, the KFC, the 'Diet Coke', the 'Pepsi', the flavourless coffee, the eternal iced water, inferior cold beer drunk from the bottle – all at cut-rate prices in stereotyped eating establishments. Take-away food and beverages enable people to eat and drink on the move, to and from work, on the street, in car, bus and subway. Frozen take-home TV dinners allow families to munch away while watching the latest screen atrocities in the comfort of their living rooms. People are constantly eating and guzzling, as junk food is becoming a national health hazard and obesity is rising. Fortunately for Americans, they can still be at home while travelling abroad since delicacies like 'Big Mac', 'Coke' and 'Bud' are now available throughout the world in globalized outlets in any of the major international cities and often in small towns.

Americans seem to be more insular and parochial than ever before, despite the fact that mounting numbers have travelled abroad. Their view of the outside world is gleaned from watching, on average, four hours of TV per day, listening to the radio, and reading a selection of magazines like *Time* and *Newsweek*, and a sadly deficient medley of regional newspapers. Even the much lauded *New York Times* and *Washington Post* offer only a glimpse of what is actually happening out there, and the editorials take a holier-than-thou attitude to the chaos they are observing. Because of their transient lives, moving frequently from city to city and from state to state, searching for jobs or for more lucrative positions and opportunities, Americans seem to be losing any sense of place, any specific geographical location that they can call their own and to which they can permanently belong. They desperately seek such a place in which to put down roots. In their flight from their peripatetic existence, the relatively affluent are beginning to turn inward, seeking refuge from life's hustle and bustle by staying at home, except for vacations in expensive resorts in and outside the United States. In many areas throughout the country, they live in three million sequestered and guarded compounds. Their homes in suburbia or in high-rise urban apartments have become castles against a hostile external environment. More and more of the well-to-do are retreating within the confines of their house or apartment, not only for entertainment but also for business. A comfortable life can be spent entirely at home, safely protected from summer's torrid humidity and winter's icy blasts, without venturing forth to the movies, theatre, concert or lecture hall, opera house, art gallery, museum, sports arena, library, restaurant or café. When they do venture forth, they whisk through the streets from underground garage to underground garage. Telephone, radio, TV, video movies, CD and DVD players, fax and answering machines, computers and take-away meals are substitutes for venturing forth into the outside world, for actually seeing people, mingling with them, and talking to them. Virtual reality for some is displacing true reality. Business can be conducted at home instead of in the office, a situation rendered possible by the amazing technology of computers, the Internet and the information highway. Why go to the office or store, when shopping and banking can be efficiently accomplished from the safe and comfortable home? Physical exercise and sunshine are readily available at home through an imposing array of machines and lamps that can easily be ordered by phone, fax or computer.

Americans might as well stay at home because of the inordinate length of time wasted in understaffed stores and banks, downsized to give soaring profits to shareholders. All of American life is becoming persistently and rapidly computerized. Banks are laying off staff, so that getting personal attention is ever more time-consuming and exasperating, and in desperation patrons turn to cash machines and telephones for transactions. In fact, some bank employees even resent their more recalcitrant customers for not using these facilities, as they dream of being relieved of such personalized tasks and made available for advancement in the managerial hierarchy. Intended to save the costs of bookkeeping, computerized cash registers in large and small retailers add to the time wasted during shopping, as does the staff's apparent inability to do even the simplest addition and subtraction without recourse to the ever present calculator. Reliance on computerization does not seem to have made routine business transactions more efficient than in the past for customers, but now mistakes can be conveniently blamed on the machine. When computers crash, business comes to a resounding halt.

Use of computers and the Internet has exploded throughout the world, launching what some perceive as a technological revolution. Five years ago, a million people in the world were using the Internet. Now the figure is at least forty million, most of them in the United States, with no end in sight. More and more Americans are turning to the web for shopping, banking, electronic mail and all kinds of information. Widespread Internet usage may well, or so we are told, help depress inflation, because individuals will surf the web looking for the cheapest commodities. Surfing the web, moreover, may also depress wages since work can be farmed out to the cheapest global source. Education can be transformed since all users have a rich source of data at their instant disposal: information about books and the books themselves, archives, bibliographies, newspapers and news articles, music, films, paintings and much else. Serious intellectual debates take place on the web. No need now to attend university in person, or at least university education can be valuably enhanced and supplemented by surfing the Internet. Whether it will replace traditional university education remains to be seen, but it is already clear that the most ardent proponents of education via the Internet seem to confuse information with thinking, reflection and critical judgment, which can only be developed and nourished through personal contact and relationships with other students and instructors. Computerization and the Internet, according to informed opinion, will further corporate interests and cement relations with comparable echelons of experts in different global business firms, facilitating solutions to common problems. It may well be true that the new technological revolution will immensely strengthen economic globalization, thus extending and solidifying a single capitalist world. But serious problems are attendant on the ever rising hours of labour, stress and tension of workers. Office and home workers are being overwhelmed by the burdensome and tedious task of simply sending and receiving countless messages from a variety of electronic sources. Which source to use and when to use it have become exceedingly vexing questions, severely taxing the patience and skill of workers, in view of the fact that the myriad messages have to be read and digested, and prompt replies have to be sent out. The technological revolution brought about by the computer and the Internet seems to have had no small part in stoking the American culture of frenzy, with untold repercussions for the psyches of the individuals caught up in it.

A number of absolutely critical interrelated problems are raised by these developments. The customary US faith in technology as the panacea for its most pressing domestic and international ills furnishes a somewhat convenient excuse for ignoring and bypassing the most urgent questions of the day. We may very well be witnessing a new technological revolution of momentous import for the future, but what of the consequences, especially those unforeseen? Have policy-makers painstakingly assessed the whole range of possible consequences? Probably not, if the wars in Afghanistan and Iraq are indicators. Washington's policy-makers seem incapable of cool, detached, rational thought on matters of this magnitude. In the cases of Iraq and Afghanistan, the tail appears to be wagging the dog,

American capitalism determining the response. Has anyone in the government given serious calculated attention to the colossal problems of feeding, clothing and housing the world's unfortunate masses, not to mention the impoverished in the United States itself? Is the latest amour with technology a further encouragement to the retreat of Americans within themselves, seeking some kind of foolproof sanctuary from the exigencies of the external world which, in the final analysis, are inescapable? This may not be true of all Americans, but as computers become cheaper, and surfing the Internet an activity increasing at breakneck pace, the incalculable consequences for the future may indeed be catastrophic.

Another question has to do with America's unrivalled world role in the so-called information industry, testimony to which is the latest list of the world's 250 billionaires today (in contrast to ninety-six in 1987). Of the top ten, three, including Bill Gates, are Microsoft dignitaries. The new technological revolution has simply promoted the global grip of American capitalism, which will further tighten throughout the world as the revolution advances, every step in its progress forwarded by its military might.

5

Our brief profile of American society must end with a few impressions of the cultural terrain in the narrow sense. To begin with, the stranglehold of capitalist tyranny on American culture cannot be better illustrated than by some statistics on the corporate control of the media. As of 1989, twenty-three corporations controlled most of the national media, down from fifty in 1982. About 80 per cent of daily newspaper circulation is in the hands of two publishing giants, Gannett and Knight Ridder, a concentration of ownership still continuing. Gannett not only owns many dailies and weeklies, but also radio and TV stations and many cable and satellite operations. Six major companies distribute virtually all magazines sold in every newsstand. Most book sale revenues flow to eleven publishers, and a few huge national bookstore chains like Borders, owned by big business complexes, have an immense distributive share. From publishing to television, where a comparable phenomenon is occurring: the major stockholders of the huge ABC and CBS are banks like Chase Manhattan, Morgan Guaranty Trust, Citibank and Bank of America. General Electric is the sole owner of NBC. Representatives of other powerful corporations are on the boards of the major networks, among them IBM, Ford, American Express, General Motors, Mobil Oil, Xerox. This kind of domination over publishing and the mass media means that money and profit are the chief motives in their functioning, and that the paramount concern is with high sales, not with the intellectual and artistic merits of the public presentations. Little attention is paid to the threat of the concentration of media ownership to freedom of speech and thought.

Entertainment, not enlightenment, is the watchword of American popular culture, and the biggest box-office attractions are the greatest earners. Sport is no longer about playing games for the sheer joy of playing, but big business for profit. A convicted felon, the professional boxer Mike Tyson, received $75 million in 1996 for just three hours of rather mediocre work in the ring. Arnold Palmer earned over $84 million, and Andre Agassi and Jack Nicklaus approached the $75 million mark. Even more extravagant remuneration was garnered by popular entertainers outside the sporting world: Oprah Winfrey with $97 million in 1996; the Beatles, $130 million in 1995–96; Michael Jackson, $90 million in the same year; and so on *ad nauseam*, with the most popular entertainers, the stars at the box office. By contrast, the median family income in the United States is about $40,000 per annum.

Hollywood has certainly left its stamp on the banal entertainment culture of the United States. The *International Herald Tribune* of 2 June 1999 reported on the queue in Westwood Village, Los Angeles, California, several days in advance, to buy tickets for the first showing there of *Star Wars; Episode I – The Phantom Menace*, following the success of three previous *Star Wars* movies. The latest *Star Wars* grossed $250 million in less than two weeks, more than any previous film. Commenting in the *New York Review of Books* (24 June 1999), Lewis Menand wrote that it 'is entertainment for eight-year old boys'. *Star Wars* topped *Titanic*'s previous record of the highest gross, 'a movie', Menand says, '(so far we have come) for ten-year-old girls'. His verdict is that 'the big Hollywood movies are mostly pitched at the audience of pre-teens'. Burhan Wazir, in the London *Observer* (20 June 1999) commented on three 'summer blockbusters': *Star Wars*, *Notting Hill* and *Austin Powers – The Spy Who Shagged Me*. He called them 'regurgitated garbage', ending his review: 'You can pay for this shit, but you sure can't watch it'.

From the ridiculous to the sublime, we turn from Hollywood and its tremendous profits to the many struggling music and arts groups throughout the country. Pop music has displaced classical music, especially among the young, as by far the dominant musical idiom. Our ears are blasted with raucous noise in shops, restaurants, bars and cafés. Nowhere can we relax in peace and quiet. The new music presented by symphony orchestras is to many listeners far from being worth hearing a second time. No Bartók, Stravinsky or Shostakovich has appeared on the musical scene. Minimalism spearheaded by John Adams can hardly carry the name of classical music: boring, repetitive, soul-destroying. Symphony orchestras are in dire financial straits, since there are virtually no public funds at their disposal. Attendance has dropped, and the energies of the orchestras' backers have to be devoted to fundraising, in particular from possible corporate donors. The story is much the same with the visual arts: federal and state subsidies are drying up. Increasingly, arts groups throughout the land are forced to pare costs, in the business lingo of the time, becoming more 'cost effective', and relying on corporate donors. Appeals for funds from private donors fall on deaf ears if the emphasis is on the vital civilizing and humanistic function of the arts. The arts have to be justified in economic terms to givers of funds. Corporate donors must be convinced that money given to the arts will eventually mean more money in their own pockets. Apart from reducing their own costs, arts organizations have to demonstrate that their pro-grammes – visual arts, opera, dance, etc. – provide an important economic stimulus, in the way of opening up new restaurants, cafés and shops. Some art groups have even decided to enter the world of private enterprise by setting up their own businesses, for instance by producing graphic designs.

The United States may boast the world's highest proportion of university and college graduates, something in the neighbourhood of 50 per cent of the adult population. Yet here again there are deeply disturbing signs on the horizon. Public funding of universities is decreasing. University administrators spend much of their time raising money, and in the meantime tuition fees are reaching such a high level that only students from affluent families can possibly afford to attend, except for the fortunate few receiving scholarships and bursaries. But there are ever more alarming developments to do with the public perception of the nature of higher education. Most stu-dents attend university 'to get a job', not for love of knowledge for its own sake, or to immerse themselves in the great cultural traditions they have inherited. As a consequence, many students and much of the public are convinced that knowledge is solely utilitarian fact-gathering. For this reason, enrolment in computer and business courses has swollen, to the detriment of the traditional arts and sciences. The former general education courses required of all students to introduce them to their rich cultural traditions have deteriorated into popularity contests for offering and enrolling in the 'sexiest' courses. The idea that higher education should foster a critical understanding of our world and hone the skills of logical thought and analysis seems to be a relic of the past. Instead we are obsessed by job training and fact collecting, a tendency that has been propelled by the new technological revolution, with the use of computers and the Internet. It is quite possible that some graduates of the better American universities have as undergraduates never been exposed to the cultural greats, to Plato and Saint Augustine, Shakespeare and Milton, to Darwin and Marx. No longer are books to be loved and cherished, only surfing the Internet. One result of the belief in knowledge as fact-gathering for the purpose of future employment has been the establishment by business concerns of corporate universities. Their aim appears to be the training of efficient, co-operative, pliable and expert workers for private enterprise.

In addition to these afflictions, universities will perhaps be suffering in other ways. By the twelfth grade secondary students are falling below their international peers in mathematics and science. After 11 September Lynne Cheney, wife of Vice-President Dick Cheney, wrote and published *America: A Patriotic Primer* (2002), designed to instil patriotic fervour in five-year-olds. She also founded the American Council of Trustees and Academics (ACTA), which seeks to purge universities of their liberal tendencies.

Of even greater concern is the recent craze for creationism. The press informs us that over 40 per cent of Americans now believe in creationism and reject the Darwinian theory of evolution, despite the fact that absolutely no scientific evidence exists for the former view. It seems to be largely the brainchild of the religious right with its powerful lobbying influence in state capitals and in Washington. Not long ago the Kansas state school board banned the mention of evolution in books used in all state schools. While in 1999 members of the Kansas school board who favoured creationism against evolution were voted out of office, Alabama, Nebraska and New Mexico have placed severe limitations on the teaching of evolution in their state schools, and Illinois, Ohio, Wisconsin, New York and Massachusetts are beginning to have serious reservations about evolution. Some 40 per cent of American Catholics now reject the theory of evolution, even though the Pope has reaffirmed the Church's commitment to it. How can students entering universities after such brainwashing possibly acquire any genuine understanding of science and the scientific? Much more disturbing is the fact that in the presidential campaign of 2000, the leading Republican candidate, and now President, approved the restrictions on the teaching of evolution, and even the Democrat, Vice-President Gore, hedged when publicly questioned on the subject. It is simply appalling that the United States, at the forefront of science and technology, should be the heartland of this kind of bigotry and superstition.

Finally, what of the university students themselves? Can any sweeping generalizations be made about their outlook and behaviour without verging on rash caricature? Their serious worries and anxieties should at the outset be recognized and stressed. Their lives are fraught with tensions, chief of which is concern about jobs after graduation, for unless they excel in their studies well-paid job opportunities seem to be relatively scarce. Moreover, they are plagued with all sorts of deeply worrisome problems. For the first time, perhaps, they are exposed to the adult world. Among their fears are AIDS, acquaintance rape, pregnancy, drug abuse, alcoholism and the ugliness of racism. Few students are well informed about world events or knowledgeable about domestic and especially international politics, relying on TV and seldom reading newspapers. Even fewer apparently buy books, except those required for their courses. Intellectual stimulus comes mainly from surfing the Internet. Afternoons may be spent watching the tube, soap operas, playing video games and trading corporate stock market shares on the Internet. Weekends usually begin on Thursday evening, and then there is the round of sorority and fraternity conviviality. Most seem to be steadfast middle-of-the-roaders in their social and political attitudes, although some volunteer to help the needy. Most have never attended protest rallies, nor do they take strong social and political positions. They are beset by all the uncertainties and tensions of contemporary life. While much of this short profile is overdrawn – there are many worthy exceptions, especially in the 'anti-capitalist' movements – at the same time it suggests the real dangers of producing a generation or more of cultural philistines, closed-minded, if not mindless, consumers of American culture in the worst sense, not ardent, questioning, open-minded, creative participants in a vibrant culture.

Can there be any doubt that American society is in decline? It appears to be a sick society: if not in the throes of a terminal illness, at least in serious need of remedial attention. A class-riven society with a culture of violence, a culture of consumerism and a culture of entertainment, this is the result of the new tyranny of capitalism. Can the United States in truth claim to be a beacon of hope and enlightenment for the rest of the world? Does it set a promising example for others to follow?

6

THE VACUITY OF POLITICS

The remarks of columnist Martin Wolf, in the *Financial Times* (15 September 1999), are worth placing in juxtaposition with those of the distinguished former diplomat and historian, George Kennan, in an interview by Richard Ullman in the *New York Review of Books* (11 August 1999). After mentioning the imperfection of the world and the United States, Wolf ends: 'This was the American century. Given the grim alternatives to US hegemony, the rest of the world should, for once, express its gratitude'. He had already maintained that the United States

is indeed the exceptional country most of its people believe it to be. Its politics are federal, its values commercial and its ideology, freedom. It is for these reasons the only very large country – large in population, resources and size – that is also rich, stable and democratic.

He continues that the United States is

> a child of Britain ... also the Enlightenment's best product, characterized by the division of church and state, by republican institutions, by the separation of powers and the rule of law. It is a country dedicated to the democratic proposition that who you are depends not on inherited status, but on personal achievement.

Kennan, in contrast, fears that the

> whole tendency to see ourselves as the center of political enlightenment and as teachers to a great part of the rest of the world strikes me as unthought through, vainglorious, and undesirable. If you think that our life here at home has meritorious aspects worthy of emulation by peoples elsewhere, the best way to recommend them is, as John Quincy Adams maintained, not by preaching at others but by force of example. I could not agree more.

Then comes the frank admission:

> We are not, really, all that great. We have serious problems within our society these days, and to the rest of the world, we should demonstrate that we are now confronting these problems with a bit more imagination, courage and resolve than has been apparent in the recent past.

About American popular culture sweeping the world, Kennan judges: 'We export to anyone who can buy it or steal it the cheapest, silliest, and most disreputable manifestations of our "culture". No wonder that these effusions become the laughing-stock of intelligent and sensitive people the world over.' On the same subject, he concludes: 'And so we must expect, I suppose, to appear to many abroad, despite our military superiority, as the world's intellectual and spiritual dunce, until we can change the image of ourselves we purvey to others.' Kennan does not contradict Wolf's rather glowing portrayal of America's economic and military global hegemony, but he is far less reluctant to face up to the serious problems within the United States, and the growing hubris accompanying the unparalleled world might of the nation. Chapter 5 has treated some of the basic social problems to which Kennan is undoubtedly alluding, and this chapter will suggest some of the serious flaws of current American politics as a counter to Wolf's optimism.

1

Perhaps if other peoples and countries only fully recognized the symptoms of illness afflicting advanced capitalist America, they might find it a far less attractive model for emulation. So many living elsewhere seem eager to transplant themselves to the United States for understandable reasons. Obviously, the average American, even the impoverished, in comparison to many in the depressed areas of the world, which means most of the global population, lives relatively comfortably and securely. The price, however, paid in mental and spiritual well-being may be exceedingly high. The lure of America to a great extent rests on the phenomenal globalization of its popular culture: the movies, the pop music, the celebrities, the sport, the 'Big Mac', the KFC, the pizza. Much of the enchantment depends upon sheer window-dressing. But once a foreigner is permanently trapped in the hectic and ruthless swirl of urban America, the reality may very well be a far cry from what was anticipated from abroad.

The 'world's greatest country', the 'indispensable nation' with the 'world's finest' armed forces are among the favourite accolades drummed into Americans at every conceivable opportunity by the media and politicians amidst flag-waving and flags flying from the homes of suburbia. These patriotic paeans of self-congratulation are an integral component of the current political, social and even religious rhetoric. The United States, of course, suffered far less than any of the other allied powers during the Second World War, incurring the fewest casualties overseas, and with a completely unscathed homeland. Yet when the US media and politicians recall that catastrophic world conflict, they often give the United States the place of honour in securing the allied victory. If acknowledged at all, the absolutely vital role of the Soviets and Chinese with their tremendous loss of lives and devastated homeland is downplayed, sometimes even omitted altogether, let alone the costly and valiant parts played by the British, French and Commonwealth nations.

In fact the United States prospered enormously from the war, was only pulled out of the depression because of it, and constructed an economy of unprecedented strength accounting for the immediate post-war boom. Today, however, after the disastrous military blunder of the costly and futile Vietnam war, the United States has become progressively more hesitant in comparison with other nations to expose its armed forces to loss of life and equipment. NATO's war with Serbia over Kosovo, the invasion of Afghanistan and the war in Iraq are examples: bomb the opponent's armed forces and infrastructure from safe high altitudes without an American life lost (though causing many civilian casualties), and, wherever possible, let others do the dangerous groundwork. The American armed forces have become, as it were, secure havens of good pay for men and women, saving them from unemployment and the uncertainties of civilian life. Seldom are they thought of as the traditional life-risking institutions. American lives, at all costs, are not to be squandered in foreign adventures. Headlines are made by a handful of lives lost and the downing of a few planes, and damning questions are raised in congressional debate. All of this seems somewhat disingenuous since the armed forces are voluntary, and peacetime conscription no longer exists. Few realize that loss of lives of servicemen and servicewomen is the necessary cost and concomitant of attaining and maintaining supreme imperial power. And yet, the US is increasingly resorting to military action to promote its imperial interests.

American hubris nearly amounts to the rewriting of history for the gullible and uninformed public. They are perpetually reminded that they should be proud citizens of the greatest democracy the world has ever known, an 'opportunity society', a 'classless meritocracy', the citadel of freedom against oppression and tyranny everywhere. Through industry and perseverance everyone is capable of scaling the social ladder, bettering themselves, if not becoming millionaires and even billionaires. No one, of course, is told that if everyone pursues this course, many will still have to do the menial labour and nasty, backbreaking jobs in a highly developed capitalist system. No answer is forthcoming as to who will do this. Except for the many at the bottom of the social pyramid, Americans live in a dreamland. It is almost as if gnawing anxiety and self-doubt are compensated for by the glossy and seductive language of self-exaltation. If these assorted boasts are repeated over and over again, Americans, at least the fortunate minority, may eventually come to believe in their veracity. For the average American has little basis from which to estimate the truth of the ceaseless promotional statements. Working long hours in possibly two or even three low-paying jobs, exhausted in the evening, with only a few moments for a beer or a Coke and the TV, he or she is abysmally informed, and seldom reads a book or an adequate newspaper. What he or she gets is pep-talk, the shouts of a cheerleader, amounting to little more than brainwashing that may move them to act as if what is being told is actually true. American 'democracy and the free market' is another popular slogan, joining the two together like Siamese twins, as if democracy had anything to do with the free market, or the latter implied the former.

Once the threat of international communism and the Soviet empire ended, the United States emerged as the single colossal superpower, the mightiest imperialist nation in human history. The ancient Roman empire and the more recent Spanish, Portuguese, Belgian, Dutch and British empires are dwarfed by comparison, both in extent and in terms of sheer force. The American empire is a true global Leviathan with no possible rival on the immediate horizon. The United States rules its planetary empire not by the conquest of territory or military power alone. While possessing military strength in abundance, American domination depends fundamentally on its vast global economic power, not so much directly on legions of soldiers, as indirectly on the gigantic international business corporations that have burgeoned since the Second World War's end. The globalization of the economy relies on the United States for peace and security and is firmly anchored in the United States.

Throughout its world empire, the United States relies on some of its most loyal imperial subjects and listening posts. The United States is sandwiched between Mexico to the south and Canada to the north, the world's largest land mass after Russia. Neighbouring Canada, with one-tenth the population of the United States, is its biggest trading partner, and hence is basically a subject nation. In each of the world's regions close links have been forged with countries that have demonstrated the keeping of the faith and that for a variety of reasons are deeply indebted to American hegemony: the United Kingdom in Europe; Israel, Turkey, Saudi Arabia and Egypt in the Middle East; South Korea, Taiwan and the Philippines in the Far East; Chile, down one side of South America and Mexico, Puerto Rico and Panama in the Caribbean and Central America. Whenever anything gets out of hand or threatens American interests in these sectors, the United States intervenes directly, as in Somalia, Iraq, and Afghanistan; or indirectly, sometimes with catastrophic results, as in Angola and formerly in Afghanistan. Or dominance over NATO can be used as an instrument of subjection, for example recently in Kosovo. In its own backyard, so zealously guarded by the 200-year-old Monroe Doctrine, the United States has not hesitated to intervene militarily, as in the midget countries of Grenada, Panama and Haiti, or by assiduously and secretly supporting the opposition, as in Nicaragua, or by subsidizing, for example, Guatemala's dictatorial regime. Nor does the United States hesitate to use assassination to end regimes contrary to its interests, as in the CIA's removal of President Allende in Chile and the installation of the pro-American tyranny of General Augusto Pinochet. The United States is an old and accomplished hand at the use of terrorism. The invasion of Cuba to remove President Fidel Castro and the CIA's attempt to assassinate him were abject failures. Indeed, the record of US domination over Central America, via the United Fruit Company, is legendary, a ruthless violation of human rights.

The case of Cuba constitutes an indelible black mark against the United States. Why such a small Caribbean island, so to speak in the American backyard, should be considered a threat to American interests, warranting a damaging economic embargo that has lasted for years, is beyond ordinary comprehension. Castro and his forces succeeded in toppling the Cuban pawn of the United States, the corrupt Batista tyranny that had made the island into a huge gambling casino and brothel for pleasure-seeking Americans. Castro managed to restore the self-respect and dignity of the Cubans, transforming their island into a vigorous state with education and health systems the envy of Latin America. Much of what he accomplished, unfortunately, has withered on the vine because of the collapse of his Soviet protector and the imposition of the American economic embargo. If anything, this embargo and the threatening attitude of the United States have bolstered Castro's regime. The animosity of the United States seems mainly a response to the pressures in Washington, mounted by the huge colony of politically dubious Cuban exiles living in Florida who have become supporters of Republican Governor Jeb Bush, brother of President Bush. Possibly more to the point, the United States could never tolerate a Cuba serving as a social model for oppressed Latin American countries.

In support of its global hegemony, the United States has its own enormous military forces and is able to dominate the United Nations, although that international body is certainly not always a rubber stamp for American policy. At a moment's notice the United States can deploy its military units, alone or as part of a UN peacekeeping force, to any trouble spot. In any one year the United States spends more (only 3 per cent of GNP) on its military forces than the annual combined budgets of Russia, China, Japan, France, Germany and the United Kingdom. Considerable influence is exerted by the United States on the UN, whose headquarters are conveniently located in New York City. Nevertheless, the United States hardly sets an admirable example to other nations in its failure to pay its debt of over $1 billion in outstanding annual membership dues, a default largely due to congressional partisan politics. When the UN needs an international peacekeeping force, America has a weighty voice in its mobilization, even though its own contribution of troops may be rather small in comparison to that of other nations. Faithfully following every twist and turn in American foreign policy is its dutiful European satellite, the United Kingdom, so loyal over Vietnam, Somalia, Iraq, Kosovo and Afghanistan. This 'special relationship' seems to hold no matter the party in power in Washington or Westminster, although Tony Blair has taken it to new extremes.

The boastful and self-congratulatory air of Americans about their accomplishments is often coupled with a bullying posture towards international friends, neighbours and allies. World diplomacy conducted in the American style, more obvious than before because of the absence of any challenge to world *imperium*, seems basically to be a reflex of domestic politics. There are grounds to wonder whether US foreign policy, besides maintaining global supremacy, is anything more than an ill-conceived hodgepodge of internal political pressures on Washington. In part to woo Polish Americans and other voters of Central European extraction, America has insisted on expanding NATO eastwards against considered expert judgment and at the risk of alienating Russia. Apart from this clumsiness, American policy towards Russia has been mean-spirited, penny-pinching and lacking in vision. No magnanimous gesture of goodwill or friendly helping hand has been extended to its fallen former rival. There has been nothing comparable to the generous (and politically astute) Marshall Plan after the Second World War. Instead, the most the United States can do is first to promote the absurd (culturally, politically and economically) project of remaking Russia overnight into a free-market capitalist society; and second, to aid and abet American capitalist enterprise in plundering the rich resources of that fallen country.

The numerous Cuban expatriates now living in Florida must be kept in the American political orbit by tightening the economic blockade of Cuba and by the inept Helms–Burton Act that seeks to prevent and penalize foreign nations doing business with Castro. Nor has the nation whose top three billionaires have more combined assets than the world's forty-eight poorest countries been generous in financial aid to those overseas areas suffering from starvation and malnutrition, AIDS and lack of education. Only 0.1 per cent of American GDP has typically been spent on foreign assistance in recent years, the lowest of any advanced capitalist country, as compared to 3 per cent at the time of the Marshall Plan. Admittedly, Americans gave huge amounts to charitable organizations, far exceeding the contributions of any other nation, but these are primarily aimed at helping those at home, not abroad. Again, one wonders why in the world's 'greatest democracy' such immense funds should be directed at its own population. All of this seems to contradict the judgment (*Financial Times*, 22 November 2001) of Lawrence Lindsey, President Bush's economic adviser and director of the White House's National Economic Council, who concludes his article: 'men and women who are free to pursue individualism and material wealth turn out to be the most compassionate of all'. This generosity bred by the dismantling of the welfare state and lower business taxes is being directed at their own kind, not outsiders.

Despite their increasing foreign travel in recent years and constant exposure to different cultures overseas, Americans, anxious to return to 'the best country in the world', can never fully appreciate what it means to be non-American. It seems only natural to many Americans that everyone in the world should wish to be like them. In their growing arrogance and lack of humility, they appear to be convinced that the whole planet should be stamped in their mould. If only the world could be completely Americanized, all its worries and troubles would soon be ended. The American dream should be the world dream, to be realized by American-dominated globalization. For instance, the typical American reaction to Canada's persistent efforts to prevent the flooding of the home market with publications from south of the border has been heavy-handed and singularly lacking in any kind of sympathetic understanding of Ottawa's difficult situation. And so the story could be repeated again and again. Pax Americana would seem to be bluster and bombast with a big stick and further unilateralism.

2

Now we move from a bird's-eye view of the American empire in the international arena to some thoughts on the core of the problem, the nature of domestic politics. The United States may be widely touted as the 'world's greatest democracy', but in reality it fails to meet the minimal substantive and procedural criteria of 'democracy' in any traditionally accepted meaning of the term (outlined in Chapter 3). Let us consider first the substantive aspects of democracy. The United States has become an increasingly inegalitarian society, with an ever widening and deepening gulf between the haves and have-nots. No let-up in this alarming development seems to be in sight. One per cent of the population today controls 40 per cent of the wealth. Equality as related to democracy does not denote levelling or absolute parity. But the broadening and deepening gap between the affluent and the poor also clearly negates the procedural democratic principles of 'one person, one vote' and the 'rule of law'. Where immense concentrations of economic power exist in the hands of a few, obviously their votes will count for much more than those of the less affluent majority, and there will be one law for the rich and one law for the poor. Political power has always been and continues to be subordinate to economic power, always at its beck and call. Equality before the law means one thing for the rich few and another for the many poor. Now, however, many of us have accepted that, aside from these procedural stipulations, equality has little to do with democracy. Equality in the economic sense has become little more than a dirty word, to be replaced by 'freedom', which to those who minimize the salience of equality, signifies freedom of business and entrepreneurship from governmental intervention and control, freedom of property acquisition, freedom of markets, freedom of consumer choice.

Freedom is obviously absolutely critical to democracy, above all freedom from discrimination because of race, colour and religious belief; freedom to associate; freedom of worship; freedom of expression in speech and print. Freedom, in sum, implies an active and forthright toleration for all those who differ from ourselves. Yet freedom is essentially a hollow concept in a society with an ever widening gulf between a decreasing number of the very rich, growing richer by the day, and a burgeoning majority of the poor and needy. Such a social situation in the final analysis seems to put paid to the attempt to enshrine American democracy. Social equality and freedom are inseparably linked. How can 'democracy' be more than a clever confidence trick under such obvious conditions of economic inequality, constantly growing, with no apparent end? And can there be any genuine freedom in such conditions? Is democracy in America, furthermore, by any stretch of the imagination an authentic sanctuary for the world's weak and unfortunate, as it was in ancient Athens, except perhaps as a means of supplying a vast pool of underpaid workers to perform the arduous menial jobs, by necessity underpinning the domination of the wealthy and relatively affluent? How can the United States possibly be identified with a meaningful democracy when a very sizeable and growing proportion of the population is ill-housed, progressively undernourished, without proper medical attention? Can a citizen-body working long underpaid hours, often forced to hold down several jobs in the struggle for survival, be at all concerned with affairs of state or the functioning of government? Can there be any prospects for democracy in a nation where human rights are often violated, far more so than in any of the other G-7 countries? According to recent reports of the United

Nations and of Amnesty International, capital punishment in most of the states, prolonged waits on 'death row', the execution of minors, and proliferating racial discrimination are distinct blots on the American humanitarian record. Yet this alarming feature of life is seldom publicized in the American press. A blind eye, moreover, is often turned to the trampling of human rights by regimes that the US supports in Central America and the Caribbean, in Saudi Arabia, Egypt and elsewhere.

Is there any chance for authentic democracy where the eligible voters are poorly informed, more so than in any other advanced industrial country, about what is actually occurring in their own country (not to mention their ignorance of world affairs), where functional illiteracy is constantly rising, annual book sales are dropping, and where the public, including university graduates, are suffering from an ever growing and disturbing historical amnesia? There seems to be a singular lack of knowledge of even the major facts of American history, let alone the history of other countries and peoples. The majority are so busy eking out a living that they have little time or energy to improve themselves educationally, except to take job-relevant courses to forward their occupational prospects. For the others, there is little excuse. They seem to be more interested in the cultivation of their bodies than their minds. The critical and analytic faculties of both the more and the less well-to-do seem to have been blunted. When people are not being entertained, those who can and cannot afford it are busy consuming in the vast array of shops. Yet one of the crucial substantive conditions for a strong and vigorous democracy is a well-informed public who relish and actively participate in the debate of public issues. Given all its advantages, the United States, with 50 per cent of its population university and college graduates, clearly ranks rather low in this regard. Obviously, something is wrong with the whole educational system when at least 40 per cent believe in creationism and reject Darwinian evolution.

If American democracy fails to pass the substantive test, what of the procedural standards, about which far less disagreement may exist? Admittedly, over the years the constitution has been procedurally 'democratized' with, for example, a directly elected Senate, abolition of state property qualifications for voting, the ending of slavery, and the granting of women's suffrage. Nevertheless, fewer than 50 per cent of eligible citizens any longer trouble to vote in presidential elections compared, for instance, to the 70 per cent turn-out in the British General Election in 1997 when the Conservatives were roundly defeated by the Labour Party under the leadership of Tony Blair, for that country the lowest turn-out since 1935. Within recent years American presidential candidates customarily win with just under 50 per cent of the ballots cast, roughly the same number as their opponents. In other words, the winner of the world's most powerful office who heads the global American empire is actually chosen by less than one-half of the actual voters or under one-quarter of those entitled to the franchise. Congressional races within the states usually yield similar statistics. So the president and the Congress, who between them enact laws binding on all Americans, represent at best 25 per cent of eligible voters. This is hardly a vibrant democracy in any procedural sense.

Why has there been such a low turn-out in recent federal elections? Many citizens are disenchanted with politics and politicians, who are often dismissed for their alleged dishonesty and corruption as simply 'smooth operators'. Perhaps with good reason, since the high level of corruption, probably no more pervasive than before, has, through the media, become much more visible to a cynical and impatient citizenry. Because of the exorbitant campaign expenses, including TV, radio and newspaper advertisements, and the inadequacy of public electoral funding, running for public office is out of the question except for rich candidates or a coterie of wealthy backers.

Other factors may be responsible for low voter turn-out. Does the electorate have clear and distinctive policy alternatives in voting for one party in preference to others? Is there any real choice between them in a land acclaimed as the fountainhead of freedom of choice? Elections are usually little more than personality contests. The average politician is an intellectual mediocrity of little foresight or keen grasp of the complex world of affairs. Survival is the *modus operandi* of the politician. Lacking strong, principled convictions, politicians are usually hypocritical fixers, power brokers, masters of flattering their supporters and constituents and at juggling facts and figures in their own favour. They are artists of the cliché and soundbite. Truth and honesty are rarely found in their words and actions. The differences that may have once separated Democrats from Republicans are rapidly disappearing. Essentially they are two wings of the same party. Both parties tend to absorb each other's policies in their efforts to capture votes and win popular approval. Few, if any, politicians venture to strike out on their own, explaining frankly and clarifying in bold, unequivocal terms the nature of the serious problems confronting America, and recommending remedial policies that are more than stop-gap measures. Congress appears increasingly to consist of like-minded legislators, frequently seeing eye to eye on basic issues, usually not so much out of conviction as in the hope of winning applause and cultivating popularity. They are often little more than the pawns of powerful interest groups: the Christian right, the tobacco lobby and the National Rifle Association. For their efforts on behalf of these and many other organizations, their palms are well greased. 'Bipartisanship', and the avoidance of 'party bickering' are, in theory at any rate, the credo of federal politics. 'Dialogue', not informed vigorous opposition, is a favourite current slogan, dialogue that proceeds by soundbite rather than the rational probing debate of the major issues. This vanishing of an authentic opposition sometimes results from voters splitting their votes, returning a president and Congress of different parties. The result is often legislative paralysis. The real culprit, however, seems to be the capitulation of both parties to the manoeuvres of capitalist enterprise.

The media, as we have stressed, are of scant help in educating the public and in mobilizing any reasonable political opposition. Except for a few notable examples, minuscule and incomplete coverage of foreign and international news is offered in the US press. This is certainly true of the capsule spectacles presented on TV, from which most viewers gain their only perception of current events. The sensibilities of the public are titillated by detailed and constant reports on the latest scandals, crimes, outbreaks of violence, and natural catastrophes like earthquakes and floods, still another instance of the inward-turning of Americans, their insular and parochial outlook. Often part of a corporate chain, newspapers frequently reflect the conservative biases of their corporate owners and chief advertisers. Public affairs TV news programmes contribute to a 'balanced debate' on national issues by presenting ostensibly opposed positions from the centre of the political spectrum, often the party spokesmen and government officials involved. The Public Broadcasting System sometimes seems little more than the propaganda arm of the Washington establishment. To score their points, politicians, officials and experts overwhelm their audience with reams of complex statistics well beyond the powers of verification and comprehension of the average individual. Sensationalism is often the only alternative. One of President Clinton's State of the Union messages to Congress had to be postponed because its televising conflicted with the Miss USA Beauty Contest; and on the evening of the delivery of the message, it was touch-and-go whether it would be completed before the announcement of the jury's verdict in the O. J. Simpson civil trial. The American public obviously does not give priority in their viewing preferences to politics, and at bottom who can really blame them?

Who then bothers to vote in the federal elections? The 50 per cent of the eligible electorate who actually vote usually have something to gain from the perpetuation of the system, or feel duty-bound as citizens of the world's greatest democracy to cast their ballots. Voters are largely, though not entirely, from the wealthy and relatively affluent and secure. The poor have been effectively disfranchised. Why should they bother to vote, caught up as they are in attempting to make a living? What difference will it make, as they see it, because politics for them is a 'mug's game'? The slick, hypocritical politicians, busily lining their own pockets in Washington, are simply incapable of addressing, much less alleviating, the deep-seated grievances that render the daily lives of the poor so nightmarish. The poor have no strong, active labour movement to fight for them against vested corporate interests, no socialist or labour party to defend them. They have no easy access to Washington politicians, as do the better-off and their highly paid lobbyists. Voting, much less active political parti- cipation, means only more of the same burdensome routine, hardly worth any effort whatsoever, unless in the highly unlikely event of the emergence of a popular spokesman, a tribune of the people.

3

Any number of pundits have commented recently on the emptiness, the banality, the strange malaise of national politics, its vacuity. In the last few years an absence of serious debate is noticeable on what might be termed the really critical national political issues. Numerous fun- damental questions in domestic and international politics require urgent attention, informed discussion and speedy resolution, but few, if any, are doing this absolutely necessary job. Politicians in the main appear to have abdicated their responsibility to confront and conduct such enquiries, and instead get side-tracked on peripheral matters, important as they are, for instance on abortion, euthanasia, gun laws, gays in the military and so on. But how do these concerns compare with vital questions, about which little is being done: an adequate universal health programme, better social security and housing, increasing impoverishment, the ever widening gap between rich and poor, electoral finances, racial discrimination, human rights, capital punishment, expansion of NATO, etc.? Voters are aware of the failure of politicians to address the most significant problems, and are no longer bothering to cast their votes. They realize that their lives will remain basically unchanged, no matter who wins. A marked decline in party loyalty may also be a symptom of the emptiness of politics. There is no serious electoral opposition to the two major political parties. And so we could go on. Quite possibly this may have changed in the last few months. While both parties gave their vigorous backing to President Bush's 'infinite war' on terrorism in the aftermath of September 11, with the recent financial scandals and drop in Wall Street share values, the Democrats have emerged from cover, and are demanding much stricter regulation of corporate activities and accounting procedures and investigation of both Bush's and Cheney's past financial dealings. There are now tentative signs of opposition to Bush's foreign policy, as the US gets bogged down in Iraq, but the Democrats have tied their own hands by supporting the President's bogus 'war on terrorism'.

How significant is the decline of American politics that seemingly has been reduced to an alarming vacuity and banality? Is it simply a passing phase, for as many point out, something similar has happened several times in the last century? Or is it something more basic and lasting? I would be more inclined to adopt the latter position, maintaining that the change is of a more permanent nature, signalling something seriously askew in American politics and society. If so, how do we account for it?

The malaise of national politics is possibly little more than the reflection of the illness plaguing American society outlined in the previous chapters, but other explanations closely connected to that illness now have to be considered under the rubrics of *economic*, *cultural* and *structural*.

The most fundamental reason for the vacuity of US politics is that so much of the citizen's life falls outside the scope of politics. The 'economy' is more, and increasingly, important in determining each person's fate. Every human practice, every social relation, is subject to the 'laws' of the economy, and more and more social functions are left to the dictates of the market, from housing to pensions.

If government and politics have finally and completely succumbed to the tyranny of capitalist enterprise, then much can be said in favour of the economic explanation of the malaise of American politics. As capitalist domination enlarges, so will the power of government shrivel, to become little more than a compliant tool of the former. Such a paralysis of government and politics and the loss of any remaining independence that they may possess seem not too far distant, given the overwhelming ideological obeisance to the idea of the free market and all that is so much at the core of the capitalist mentality directing American society. These tendencies are reinforced by the failure of any true and vigorous political opposition to arrive on the scene and by the mediocrity and failure of nerve of politicians. It should be emphasized, however, that such political and governmental servility results solely from lack of will to do otherwise, and this lack of will arises from the failure to understand critically the dire circumstances in which the country finds itself. Of course, all of this may have changed with the recent revelations of financial scandals and the slump on Wall Street. Only time will tell.

Another reason that can be given for the vacuity of American politics has to do with the quality of its popular cultural life, so sedulously fostered and promoted by capitalists as an immense source of profits. The United States has degenerated into a vast entertainment society. Everything and every action must be entertaining, even schooling and higher education. Even when the TV was screening some of the horrors of the war in Iraq, the latest sports scores were shown at the bottom of the screen. People are more interested in being perpetually entertained, excited and stimulated by what they see and hear in the media than in analysing and thinking about the urgent problems affecting their lives. Everyone is accustomed to the sensationalism that has replaced the news.

Any foreign news has virtually disappeared from the screen. The public is obsessed by the televising of celebrity trials. This was why the sexual scandal dogging President Clinton was so avidly followed in its detailed and lurid, highly publicized news and media coverage. Far less attention has been given to the much more serious crimes of the Bush administration, the lies it has told to justify war, or the personal financial interests that are at the centre of the government's policies. Small wonder that politics and political issues fail to arouse the public and to ignite their feelings; for politics, given the craven quality of most contemporary politicians, can be quite unexciting, repetitive and boring, certainly not entertaining. The malaise of national politics may also stem from the fact that the truly exciting political issues are being closely scrutinized and heatedly debated not in Washington but by a narrower concerned public at the state and local levels of government, by committees that believe they have a genuine stake in questions about schools, the environment and transportation. These may not be the entertaining discussions found on TV, but they are full of meaning to those participating.

Finally, the malaise afflicting national politics may in part be accounted for by exceedingly important structural reasons. Few, if any, today dare criticize that 'holy of holies', the constitution of the United States and the governmental system offered by the Constitutional Convention in 1787 and ratified in 1789, over two centuries ago. Many would say that any criticism of the basic law of the land is utter blasphemy. Nevertheless, certain of its very obvious defects need to be emphasized after our 200-year experience of it. The US constitution was the remarkable brainchild of the European Enlightenment. In the late eighteenth century the government of the United States launched by the constitution was a highly original and ingenious mechanism carefully designed, by means of the separation of powers with an elaborate arrangement of checks and balances on the three branches (legislative, executive, judicial), to guarantee responsible government and the rule of law, to impede tyranny from above and below, to safeguard the person and property, and immediately following its ratification, to secure through amendments the rights of freedom of speech, assembly and religion. And the constitution established not simply a national federal government, but also a federal system of state governments, so necessary for such a huge territorial expanse. The US constitution was not the first written constitution, but it was the first actually to found a government, one that has lasted for more than two centuries, and is now about the same age as the Athenian democracy and the Roman republic after the Punic Wars, neither of which possessed written constitutions. For a pre-industrial and agrarian society, the constitution initiated an amazing governmental system planned to endure, in spite of the shortcomings of those who might operate it. When it was devised and implemented the functions were exceedingly few in number; laws were far shorter in length and much less complex and technical in nature than those of today; and law-making was minimal, compared to our own legislative mills.

We should never forget, moreover, that the constitutional fathers were, by and large, dedicated republicans, not democrats. The aim of the drafters was to create a republic, not a democracy. They acutely feared and distrusted direct rule of the people, or any form of majority rule; and they sought to prevent the tyrannical rule of one person or group of individuals. Federal officials (president, vice-president, senators and Supreme Court justices) were not to be chosen by direct popular majority vote, although the input of *vox populi* would exist through the House of Representatives, whose members would be popularly elected in the states, subject originally to property qualifications on the franchise. Ancient Athenian democracy was the *bête noire* of the founding fathers, as it was to most of the historical commentators upon whom they relied. Since they never intended to fashion a democracy, their model of good government was the ideal of the 'mixed constitution' of classical antiquity, and the historical example of the ancient Roman republic, at least as they understood it. The US constitution in practice only became procedurally democratized (in part) in a lengthy historical process. All of this has to be painfully spelled out, because one of the great popular myths of our time, if people even think about it, is that the constitution from its very inception was democratic, and that the government of the United States, consequently, is the world's oldest democracy.

Aside from the intentions of the framers of the constitution, a possibly more significant question should be addressed. Even with its democratizing modifications over the years, the basic republican structure with its separation of powers and checks and balances remains much as it was. Whether this structure, conceived during the eighteenth-century Enlightenment, is at all adequate to cope with present exigencies and problems must be squarely confronted. Is it suitable for an advanced industrial capitalist nation of vast territory and population with all its social and economic complexities, and the problems of being the most powerful imperialist power ever known? To put it baldly and simply, the constitution of the United States appears to be antiquated and outdated, an antediluvian system of government that is simply inadequate to handle the many urgent problems that are faced at the opening of the twenty-first century. Among other difficulties, it has become almost impossible for such a cumbersome governmental mechanism to act efficiently, rapidly and decisively. A fusion of the legislative and executive branches in some species of parliamentary government with highly disciplined political parties and a separation of chief executive and head of state might be far better able to manage effectively and swiftly the pressing affairs of state. How would such a system have handled the Clinton–Lewinsky scandal? Perhaps the inadequacy of the central republican structure of American government helps in part to explain the paralysing political malaise besetting the United States.

4

The depressing condition of American politics can be illustrated by the emergence of the Christian right as a powerful voice on the national scene, by the protracted spectacle of the attempt to remove Bill Clinton from office, and by the experience so far of Bush's presidency. Recently, the ageing and still popular evangelist, Billy Graham, has attempted to give a clear and simple explanation for the increasing violence and disunity of American life. Having become the planetary superpower, he tells us, the United States is now the Devil's principal target. The Devil is the cause of America's vexing problems. To ward off and secure ourselves against the Devil's onslaught, Graham claims, we must purify ourselves by returning to religion and strengthening our Christian beliefs and values. In the last few years, the extreme conservatism and religious fundamentalism of the Christian right, aiming to combat the Devil's insidious assault (in the guise of a perniciously growing liberalism) on all that America most treasures, has made telling inroads into the Republican Party in the south and in suburbia across the country to Los Angeles and the northwest. Better organized than the Democrats, the Christian right has succeeded in exerting a stranglehold on the Republicans because of its skills in manipulating the electoral primaries for the selection of Republican candidates for office.

The policies advocated by the Christian right, with exceptions, are so antiquated as to be ludicrous, if they were not dangerous. The upholders of these views claim to be conservative, 'pro-American', devout Christians, deeply worried by what they label the widespread 'moral decline' of the country. They stress the importance of church affiliation and churchgoing and partially through their efforts the United States has by far the highest church attendance and the highest number of those professing a belief in God of any of the advanced capitalist countries. Religious (Christian) instruction and prayer in public schools should be mandatory, they say. The well-worn slogan of family and family values is one of their priorities, which obviously means a patriarchal family, headed by a father and husband, with a credo of Christian fundamentalism: common Bible reading and prayers before meals. Opposition to abortion as the wrongful taking of life is also essential, but like so many pro-lifers they support capital punishment – 'an eye for an eye' – and the gun lobby of the National Rifle Association, thinking that citizens have a right to bear firearms in a misinterpretation of the US constitution. Among other beliefs is a vehement condemnation of male and female homosexuality, and of feminism. As far as politics is concerned, they tend to be apolitical when it suits their purpose, latent if not outright isolationists. The less government the better; and the lower taxes the better. Capitalism and the free market are unreservedly praised as manifestations of the individualism they so exalt. Even the mildest capitalist governmental intervention to prevent excesses is branded liberalism, socialism or, even worse, communism, and becomes the focus of their wrath. Unions are also excoriated as interferences in individual freedom. Among the most sinister aspects of their perspective is an underlying racism. Whites are clearly the best, and anti-Semitism always lurks beneath the surface of the outlook – although support for Israel and its worst current policies has become an article of faith.

A disturbing element of their ideology is that their interpretation of the Bible and the Christian faith, so narrow and one-sided, represents little more than the grossest of caricatures. Their Christianity is largely derived from the fiery prophets of the Old Testament. Little, if any, inspiration comes from the social gospel of Christ, from the Sermon on the Mount, or from the humane compassion and fraternity of Christ himself and his disciples. Instead of their calls for brotherly love and turning the other cheek, we get the harsh and inhumane patriarchalism and sexism of the fire and brimstone teachings of the Old Testament. The Christian right should be supremely conscious that their highly selective and rigid interpretation of the Scriptures is by no means the sole and correct theological interpretation. Their potpourri of social and political attitudes rests on a myopic reading of the Scriptures and a misinterpretation of Christianity. They seem to be completely unaware that other readings are possible, such as Christian socialism. This doctrine, rooted in the New Testament and the teachings of Christ, taking issue with many of the precepts of the Christian right ideology, has had an incalculable influence on British politics in the last 150 years, and on the English-speaking world, especially Canada.

Possibly the most perturbing aspect of the Christian right and its insidious influence is not only its irrational set of beliefs and social and political opportunism, but also its recent impact on Washington. Some of the most prominent public figures in the congressional deliberations on President Clinton's impeachment, like the Special Prosecutor, Kenneth Starr; Congressman Robert Barr; the Chair of the House Judiciary Committee, Henry Hyde; and the thirteen House Managers of the impeachment process in the Senate, all Republicans, have very close links with it.

Whether the Christian right will prosper remains to be seen. Some early signs of breaches in their phalanx may be looming. A report in the *International Herald Tribune* of 19 February 1999, may or may not have signalled a change. The news account at any rate nicely illustrates the dangers of the irrationality of Christian right attitudes. According to the *International Herald Tribune* report, Paul Weyrich, head of the Free Congress Foundation, and for thirty years a foremost purveyor of Christian right-wing opinions, in a letter on the foundation's web site created a firestorm on the right by declaring that the culture war has been lost and that he no longer believes 'there is a moral majority'. In the letter, quoted in the article, Weyrich states:

> Politics itself has failed. And politics has failed because of the collapse of the culture. The culture we are living in becomes an ever-wider sewer. Suffice it to say that the United States is very close to becoming a state totally dominated by an alien culture, an ideology bitterly hostile to Western culture.

Again, Weyrich refers to 'a cultural collapse of historic proportions, a collapse so great that it simply overwhelms politics'. He suggests that the efforts by 'conservatives' to win the Republican presidential nomination are doomed (a prophecy which was soon proved wrong), and that they are anxious about the ever greater popular support for

Clinton during the impeachment process. General moral decline is a primary concern of conservatives. How can we be sure that our children are not 'infected'? Some kind of 'guarantee' to prevent this from happening is sorely needed. Home schooling is a remedy proposed by Weyrich: 'We need to drop out of this culture, and find places, even if it is where we physically are right now, where we can live godly, righteous and sober lives.' The article concludes by saying that many conservatives disagree with Weyrich's surrender, one of them being the distinguished former judge, Robert Bork, who insists that the conservative struggle must go on, blaming liberalism for the nation's moral decline.

A second striking example of the malaise of American politics, related to the fulminations of the Christian right, is Congress's protracted attempt to impeach President Clinton. Whatever else may be said about the Republican Congress's lengthy failure, solely on that basis Clinton's name will be inscribed in the annals of the American republic. The whole affair disrupted weighty legislative business for months, provided, initially at least, riveting entertainment for the American people, was a field-day for the media, and made the United States the laughing stock of the world. The details of the legislative process that culminated in the President's victory will be chronicled in detail and analysed minutely for years to come. The media, of course, did exceedingly well at the beginning of the process, but as days and months passed, the public became increasingly disenchanted by the interminable, boring procedures, and turned elsewhere for their entertainment.

President Clinton's relationship with Monica Lewinsky was a very personal and private one, just the kind to arouse scandalmongers and the scandal-obsessed public. Regardless of the moral rights and wrongs of the liaison and its aftermath, nothing done by the President seems to have placed the United States or the constitution in jeopardy. The considered opinion of most scholars and legal experts is that he did not even come close to violating the constitution's prescription warranting impeachment: the committing of a 'high crime or misdemeanour', imperilling the public interest. Far from being a balanced and reasonable document describing constitution-threatening behaviour, the Kenneth Starr report, on which the legislators relied, is clearly biased and partisan, filled with salacious details. With close right-wing connections, Starr and his staff appear to have performed a number of actions that imply their own wrongdoing. They succeeded in spending over $40 million in public funds on a five-year investigation, all to little avail, since none of the Arkansas financial dealings allegedly implicating the President proved to be significant, and by the time of the congressional process of impeachment the Paula Jones case had been settled. If any good can be said to have come from the whole affair, it was perhaps to cast doubt on the intentions of the Special Prosecutor, Kenneth Starr, the way he was selected and the danger of the office of the Special Prosecutor, an institution that will probably be terminated. On the debit side is further convincing evidence of the moral corruption of the Republican-dominated Congress, and above all on the complete vacuity and banality of American politics. All pressing legislative matters had to be set aside during the impeachment process.

At the very commencement of the interminable hearings, Hillary Clinton's judgment was probably the correct one, that they constituted a right-wing conspiracy to destroy the President. The House of Representatives' Judiciary Committee proceedings leading to the President's indictment was obviously a right-wing Republican partisan onslaught to get the President at all costs. The Committee was dominated by white, male, southern Republicans, many of whom were closely affiliated with the Christian right. They tended to be hypocritical – the old, old story of the pot calling the kettle black –

since during the sessions the press revealed that several of its members were guilty of sexual indiscretions in the past, not the least being the chairman, Henry Hyde. Other members, like Robert Barr of Georgia, had close ties with white supremacist groups, as did Trent Lott of Mississippi, the Senate majority leader, not a member of the Committee. It may have been that President Clinton, aside from his relationship with Monica Lewinsky, symbolized all that was so hated by the Christian right and conservative Republicans: above all, his being of the sixties generation, which, as they saw it, violated all that was sacred about American culture including racism. Moreover, the congressional Republicans tended to be politically less than astute, for as they pursued their course, they bored the American people, and possibly alienated potential voters in the elections of 2000. Regardless of President Clinton's behaviour, which the public condemned, they gave overwhelming support to his presidency, something the Republicans had not reckoned on, especially in the midterm of his final term of office.

One of the most disturbing aspects of the whole episode was the 'holier than thou' attitude of the two leading national newspapers: the *New York Times* and the *Washington Post*. Their editorializing consistently refused to dig very deep or to reveal the hearings for what they were, a rather tawdry exposé that had little bearing on the substance or dereliction of government except to delay congressional deliberations on a backlog of urgent legislation. Far more was revealed briefly and concisely in the London press (the *Guardian* and, especially, the *Observer*) about the sinister implications of the impeachment saga. Politics had been transformed from serious consideration of the critical issues of government into a carousel of sexuality. No wonder that the world's reading public shook its head in disbelief, speculating as to whether or not the United States had lost its sanity. Clinton may have been revealed as a sexual scoundrel, but the trial in the Senate rejected both articles of indictment drawn up and presented by the House, thus vindicating him as President. Unfortunately, the severity of the damage resulting from the inept and hypocritical Republican rampage to crucify him has been incalculable and may have a lasting negative impact upon American politics. Whatever the outcome, history undoubtedly will deliver a harsh verdict on the Republicans and their 'Management Committee' of thirteen, led by Henry Hyde, which introduced the bill of indictment in the Senate. Even more puzzling is the fact that congressional Republicans have failed to learn their lesson from the fiasco. After the recent spate of killings in Colorado, Georgia and Texas which raised a furore throughout the nation, the Congress, many of whose members are in thrall to the National Rifle Association, first rejected a gun control law, and then, backing down in response to an irate, pro-testing public, finally passed an exceedingly weak law. The Republicans, many of whom are identified with the Christian right, obviously do not care about the judgment of posterity.

A third and even more striking instance of the ever more vacuous condition of American politics is the victory in the presidential election of 2000 of George W. Bush, Governor of Texas, over the Democratic candidate, Vice-President Al Gore, and the nature of the Bush administration. The details are well known, but some need highlighting. Bush is the son of former President George Bush, who after one term in office was defeated by President Clinton. Under the elder Bush, US forces invaded Iraq in Operation Desert Storm, but stopped short of toppling Saddam Hussein. Under George Bush, Dick Cheney, a congressman, was Secretary of Defense and General Colin Powell was Armed Forces Chief of Staff. Both Bushes are Texas oil millionaires, as is Cheney. Serious questions have been raised, even in Congress, about the younger Bush's directorship of Harken and also Cheney's association with Halliburton, another powerful energy company, which has a substantial interest in the occupation of Iraq. George W. Bush is Yale-educated with an M.B.A. from Harvard, has very seldom travelled abroad, preferring his Texas ranch, and has little knowledge or understanding of the world at large. As a young man, he took hard drugs and was an alcoholic, and he is now a born-again Christian. His governorship of Texas was undistinguished except for his failure to contain oil refinery pollution, one of the worst in the country, and his approval of 150 executions, more than in any other state.

In the presidential election Bush lost the nation-wide popular vote to Gore, but, with the help of some dubious practices, managed to scrape through with more electoral college votes than his Democratic opponent. The crucial state in the contest was Florida, whose Governor Jeb Bush is George W.'s younger brother, and whose Secretary of State oversaw the elections. Because of the lack of uniform voting procedures and ballots, and the disfranchisement of many blacks including previously convicted felons, most of whom would have voted Democrat, the election resulted in Bush's victory, a decision upheld by the US Supreme Court, the majority of the justices being arch-conservatives. Even though the voting problems in Florida do not seem yet to have been resolved, the outcome amounted to a coup by right-wing Republicans including the Christian right, and business interests, especially the great energy corporations.

The Bush administration is closely connected with and deeply indebted to large corporate interests which contributed far more to his campaign than to Gore's. The top people holding office under Bush are clearly right-wing 'hawks', firmly embedded in the business community. Vice-President Cheney, after his stint in Congress and as the elder Bush's Secretary of Defense, became chairman and CEO between 1995 and 2000 of Halliburton, the huge Texas-based international energy corporation. Secretary of Defense Donald Rumsfeld, his Under-Secretary Paul Wolfowitz, and Secretary of the Army Thomas White, had close ties to business. White was an executive in Enron, whose financial scandals have caused such consternation. Colin Powell, Secretary of State, appears to be a moderating influence, but a hawk, Richard Perle, is one of his departmental advisers, and John Negroponte, Ambassador to the United Nations, was a mastermind of the suppression of Central American radicalism. Condoleezza Rice, former Provost of Stanford University, a right-wing academic establishment, is the National Security Adviser; and John Ashcroft, a right-wing Christian activist and one of the chief advocates of the impeachment of President Clinton, is the Attorney-General, heading the Department of Justice. Right-wing 'think tanks' like the American Heritage Foundation and the Cato Institute have come to the fore. And in the background is the Federalist Society in Washington, a rightist group that includes Kenneth Starr. One has the distinct impression that George W. Bush is simply the front man for Vice-President Cheney.

Policy-wise the Bush administration is confused, contradictory and unilateralist. Its self-proclaimed policy is laissez-faire, free-trade, deregulation, lower personal income tax and corporate tax, balanced budgets, in general the less government the better, and greater personal freedom. In practice, it has greatly expanded federal government power, raised tariffs on steel (from Europe) and softwood lumber (from Canada), increased subsidies to farmers, and is responsible for one of the greatest budget deficits in history, which is growing massively as the costs of occupying Iraq mount. It is doing nothing about air pollution and the environment, indeed relaxing regulations now in place, nothing about electoral finance reform, nothing about gun laws, nothing about drug abuse, nothing about healthcare or housing. Foreign policy is a shambles, nowhere more transparently than in Iraq, while efforts to achieve peace in Israel–Palestine are condemned by the government's strong support for Sharon against Arafat (to win the growing right-wing Jewish vote and Christian right in the US), thus further alienating world Muslims. All of this and more is compounded by the failure to do anything about foreign aid and a gung-ho attitude towards international friends and allies, offering a doctrine of pre-emptive military strikes and warfare. America is willing to go it alone, and if other countries do not like it, what can they do to rein in the world's only superpower?

The American people were obviously disillusioned by Bush as President and by at least some of his policies, for in the latter part of August 2001 opinion polls gave him only a 40% rating, one of the lowest on record for a new president with less than two years in office. And then Bush and his administration were saved by, almost literally, a bolt from the blue. Bin Laden and Al-Qaeda struck the World Trade Center in New York and part of the Pentagon in Washington in the horrific attack of 11 September. The United States was placed on a war footing, and Osama bin Laden and Al-Qaeda were linked with the so-called 'Axis of Evil' (North Korea, Iran, Iraq). After about two months Afghanistan was invaded and bombed with allied co-operation and military support. The 'infinite war' against terrorism had been launched, with no end in sight. Bush and his associates may very well have capitalized on 11 September to boost his opinion rating and to unify the nation, which rose in patriotic fervour in support of him. If true, it was an extremely clever ploy, a prime example of 'Sallust's Theorem' (see Chapter 3 above) perhaps merged with Aristotle's original precept that an external threat can be fabricated by a shrewd statesman in order to unify the people and refurbish his standing with them.

Whether the American bombing of Afghanistan was motivated less by terrorism than by clearing the way for the construction of an oil pipeline through the country to Pakistan is a moot point.

Momentarily, at least, the US managed to rally international backing and destroyed the Taliban, but failed in its original stated objective of eliminating bin Laden and Al-Qaeda, many of whose members fled to Pakistan. Ironically, before 11 September, Taliban leaders had visited Bush in Texas and were possibly negotiating the pipeline through their country. It is well known that Pakistan and the US had long before aided the country's war lords against the Soviet Union and helped the Taliban. Following the successful invasion, substantial US aid to Afghanistan failed to materialize and much of the dirty groundwork was performed by America's allies. In the United States itself, security measures were given top priority, and a cabinet Department of Homeland Defense was proposed. Civil rights were eroded in the name of security, and at least 1,000 prisoners captured in Afghanistan were held incommunicado in appalling conditions in 'Camp X-Ray' at the Guantánamo Naval Base in Cuba, perhaps a warning to Castro. Throughout all this the Democrats closed ranks with the Republicans and offered little or no opposition or criticism of the President's moves.

Before the first anniversary of 11 September, Bush's honeymoon with the American people appeared to be coming to an end with the revelations about the fraudulent corporate financial practices of Enron and the exposure of the powerful company of auditors, Arthur Andersen. In quick succession, one after the other, gigantic companies followed: WorldCom, Xerox, Merck and many others. The past financial dealings of Bush and Cheney were being investigated. The Democrats had come to life prior to the midterm elections in November 2002, and there quickly followed a continuing slump in the stock market. Consumer confidence waned, and the projected budget deficit was enormous. While the popularity of Bush was high, confidence in his handling of the economy had sagged to just over 50 per cent and seemed to be falling. What was in store for the Bush regime now? Perhaps an invasion of Iraq, which had been on the books for many months if not years, would serve once more to rally and unify Americans. Was this another example of Sallust's theorem? It is, perhaps, a hopeful sign that, as this book goes to press, Bush's ratings seem to be returning to their pre-September 11 levels, thanks to the fiasco in Iraq.

The tyranny of advanced capitalism in the United States imposes its will and discipline initially in the workplace. Then it penetrates and seizes control over the political apparatus. The victim of capitalist tyranny, America is neither substantively nor procedurally a democracy in any very meaningful sense of the term. 'One person, one vote' hides the fact that dollars mean more than votes. 'Equality before the law' means in practice that the rich are above the poor. Government has been increasingly subjected to the rule of capitalist tyranny. Political domination is exercised by the propertied in proportion to their wealth. The most materially indebted to the capitalist system determine public policy and its implementation. The two major political parties have become much the same. No vigorous, intelligent and informed political opposition any longer exists. Politics seems to have been emasculated, rendered into a free market of slogans for the trading of favours and the advancement of private interests. Burning social and governmental issues are casually shunted aside, and political discourse has degenerated into the exchange of trivia. Obfuscation rather than enlightenment has rendered politics an empty and banal exercise. Politicians in the main are mediocrities deficient in foresight, will and intelligence whose chief skill is the assiduous reading of opinion polls and the cues of focus groups, the demands of their most affluent constituents taking precedence over others. America is a class society under the mastery of the few rich and relatively affluent beneficiaries of capitalism who manipulate the levers of power over a majority of the far less secure and far less affluent without whose mental and physical labour the capitalist system would collapse. Capitalist tyranny, however, exerts its ruthless and unchallenged suzerainty not solely over the economic and political spheres. Capitalist logic and discipline seep into and influence every facet of our lives, affecting not only what we do but also how we think. The media, schools and universities assure that the values, beliefs and attitudes without which capitalism would be impotent shape our thoughts and actions. Short shrift is given to any dissent. The capitalist mentality, the indispensable soulmate of capitalist enterprise, blinds us to the possibility of any alternative, rejecting all ideas and ideals of a better future as dystopian fantasies. The only realizable future is much the same, for there appears to be no feasible alternative on the horizon.

7

CONCLUSION: A POSSIBLE ALTERNATIVE

The relentless tyranny of advanced capitalism in the United States now appears to have free rein in the absence of any imminent external threat, and with the ever expanding globalization of American capitalism and the consolidation of an unrivalled world empire. A crucial question for the future concerns the ideological buttress of capitalism's tyrannical system. How much longer can such an insidious mode of social domination possibly survive, one predicated on greed for money and possessions, transforming these into the most cherished and eagerly sought-after, though artfully camouflaged, social ideals? What can be the future of a society and culture rapidly degenerating into a collection of furiously contending profit seekers and would-be profit seekers? How can the ideological newspeak so integral to the ingeniously cultivated capitalist mentality possibly hold together such a conflux of self-seeking and pleasure-bent atoms? The tyranny of American capitalism may well prove to be self-destructive, a disastrous experiment with power.

Of course, after the recent financial scandals and the Wall Street downturn, capitalist tyranny certainly appears to be hard pressed, but is by no means in retreat or on the verge of collapse. There may be a Republican defeat in the presidential race in 2004 and an interlude of a few years or more during which capitalist operations and conduct will be less blatant and assured and more tentative and hesitant. But given the fact that Americans have been so imprinted with the capitalist mentality, no fundamental change is likely – unless a monumental crash in Wall Street brings everything down with it – and so the process will probably grind on relentlessly with a repetition of the same problems, as American society further decays and capitalist tyranny strengthens and extends its hold. The prospect is too horrifying to contemplate.

Is it too late for any kind of change of direction in the hazardous course on which American society and government have unwittingly embarked? It may be too late, for too many have too much at stake in the present to worry about the future.

What is to be done? Can anything be done? Perhaps we can find inspiration and a model in what happened in western Europe after the Second World War. A constitutional convention might be called to design a new constitution adequate for the twenty-first century and beyond. A concerted effort might be made to reform capitalism, to rebuild the welfare state, to reduce the emphasis on the virtues and efficiency of private over public enterprise. Universal medical care might be instituted along with better housing and education, strict gun control laws, improved public transport and environmental safeguards. On the foreign front, vigorous support for the United Nations and a vast increase in foreign aid might all be a beginning, along with an end to unilateralism, and instead close consultation and collaboration with foreign friends and allies. Much of this stops short of true democracy, but is a step in that direction. Above all, we must put paid to the myth that the American way of life is the ideal for the rest of the world to emulate.

If we can overcome our distaste for history and critical self-reflection, careful scrutiny of the historical record and contemplation about what it yields may stimulate our thinking and release our creative energies. At the outset, the sceptic will undoubtedly ask: in our world today what feasible alternative is there but more of the same, advanced capitalism with its cherished goal of a free society? In response perhaps we should become more sensitive to the many different types of social organization to be gleaned from the examination of the past. None of these may prove to offer satisfactory or practicable social ideals that can be effectively activated in current circumstances. History, however, is not a ragbag of social examples to be mindlessly emulated. The past is rather a repository of wisdom from which we may be able to draw sustenance and benefit in speculating about a possible future.

In very broad brushstrokes, another alternative to the tyranny of capitalist America comes to mind, in some respects its polar opposite: a society that highly values co-operation and compassion for the weak, deprived and unfortunate, at the same time not completely devaluing competition and conflict. Such a society takes every possible measure to safeguard the natural environment, following the advice and precepts of modern science. Never should nature be exploited and despoiled simply to satisfy our short-sighted cravings for gain in the present with no thought to the consequences for the future. Such a society devalues money, moneyed interests, and the acquisition of possessions. Such a society is genuinely dedicated to the eradication of poverty, disease and ignorance, instead of sweeping these tenacious and ever present problems under the carpet as we are so often prone to do. Such a society aims at the mental and bodily improvement of all. Such a society places a far greater premium on a generous, humane equality than on a thoughtless self-centred free-dom. Such a society is wholeheartedly committed to the full realization of the potentialities of each and every member, regardless of age, gender, race, creed or occupation. Such a society is self-critical about its past, present and possible future, casting off the fetters of self-deception and self-delusion. In sum, such a society is both rea-sonable and reasoning in outlook and conduct, clearly recognizing that its destiny is ultimately always in its own hands, exercising a will and determination to change for the better.

The obvious problem is whether American capitalist society can or ever will desire to proceed along the road of this possible alternative. The interests in not doing so may be too entrenched, too firmly established, the rot too ingrained, the inertia too overwhelming for any substantial alteration of direction. We have suggested the ends of a society more appropriate for authentic human beings than for the subjects of capitalism's tyranny. Ends can be easily asserted, but the crucial question is whether they can be realized. What is the mechanism of action by which they can be fulfilled? These social goals will not be delivered as a gift from political leaders. It will require concerted popular struggles. If there is a will for change, a way of achieving those ends will be worked out. In this case, however, the ends are so opposed to capitalism and its tyranny that a superhuman effort seems necessary. Supreme self-sacrifice, prodigious labour and determined, persevering co-operation over a long time are required for any major and meaningful social transformation.

In fact, we have been sketching the goals of a humane and democratic socialism. Only through the replacement of capitalist tyranny by such a socialism will humans be freed from their self-centred and greedy aggrandisement – so fruitless for most – and become able to realize themselves. Only thus will a genuine democ-racy be firmly established. The overthrow of capitalist tyranny by socialism and the establishment of authentic democracy will be a long and arduous task requiring courage and determination, insight and intellect. Not the least part will be the exposure of the capitalist mentality, the ideological tissue of lies and half-truths supporting capitalism's tyranny.